# THE INDIAN CRAFTSMAN

# THE INDIAN CRAFTS-MAN

BY

ANANDA K. COOMARASWAMY, D.Sc.

GYAN

*Published by*

GYAN

Gyan Publishing House
5, Ansari Road
Daryaganj, New Delhi-110002
Phone: 011-47034999, 9811692060
E-mail: books@gyanbooks.com

*Distribution Network*
gyanbooks.com
India, USA, Canada, UK, Australia, France



ISBN : 978-81-212-1302-8 (PB)
First Published, 1909

2nd Impression 2021

*Printed at:* Gyan Press, Delhi.



**The Indian Crafts-Man**
Author: Ananda K. Coomaraswamy

# THE INDIAN CRAFTSMAN : BY ANANDA K. COOMARASWAMY, D.Sc.

Author of "Mediæval Sinhalese Art."
With a Foreword by C. R. ASHBEE, M.A.

PROBSTHAIN & CO.,
41, GREAT RUSSELL ST., LONDON, W.C.
1909

# CONTENTS.

# APPENDICES.

# FOREWORD.

DR. COOMARASWAMY'S study of the Indian craftsman raises questions of the widest and deepest interest, questions that will not only give consciousness to modern Eastern thought, but help us with some of the most advanced of our Western problems. He tells us of a condition of life among the eastern Aryans that still exists, and he tells it in such a way as to make us feel that there is no reason why it should not go on existing. Why, we ask, has this custom of the centuries, which seems so reasonable in the East, and through which the western Aryan once passed, changed in one part of the world and not in the other, and what are the merits of the change?

If we examine our own Western economic history, more particularly the history of England, we find that the break up of the conditions of English craftsmanship and the English village order, cannot be traced back beyond the industrial revolution of the 18th century, and the enclosure of the common lands that accompanied it. Fundamentally, with us the great change came with the introduction of industrial machinery, and the question which forces itself upon us, when we look at the picture Dr. Coomaraswamy draws, is: What are the benefits to our culture of the industrial machinery that has acted in this manner?

Trained as we are to measure everything by a mechanical standard, it is difficult for us to see things clearly, to get a correct focus. We are apt to forget that our view is biassed, that we attach a disproportionate value to the productions of machinery, and that a vast number, perhaps 60 per cent., of these productions are not, as is generally supposed, labour-saving, health-giving and serviceable to our general life and culture, but the reverse. "It is questionable," said John Stuart Mill half a century ago, "whether all the labour-saving machinery has yet lightened the day's labour of a single human being"; and the years that have followed his death seem not only to have further borne out his statement, but the people themselves who are being exploited by mechanical conditions are beginning to find it out.

For machinery is only a measure of human force, not an increase of it; and it is questionable whether, owing to the abuse of machinery, the destruction and waste it brings may not equal the gain it yields. Wonderful are the great ships, and the winged words from one side of the globe to the other, wonderful is the consciousness that comes to us from those things, and from rapid movement, and from our power of destruction, but we may pay even too high a price for the boon of progress. It behoves us to ask, at least, what the price is, and if it be a fair one. Perchance, in our thoughtlessness we have, like the boy in the fairy tale, bartered away the cow for a handful of beans; well, there may be much virtue in the beans, but was not the cow good too? A more reasonable view of life and the progress of Western civilization is making us see that the pitiful slums of our great cities are not a necessary corollary to the great ships; that a nicer, saner regulation of industry will mean that the rapid displacement of human labour, and the misery it brings, may be graduated and softened; that it is not necessary for 30 per cent. of the population to die in pauperism, as is the case in England at present; that it is shortsighted and unwise to paralyze invention and skiil and individuality by unregulated machine development, and that our present gauge of the excellence in all these things—their saleability—cannot possibly continue to be a permanent gauge.

It is when Western civilization is brought face to face with the results of other cultures, Eastern cultures, when the stages of its progress are resumed from the points of view of other religions, when Japan, for instance, rejects or chooses what she needs to make her a fighting force, when India seeks to form, out of an imposed educational system, a political consciousness of her own; when Persia and Turkey are in the act of creating constitutions on the Western model, that we in the West come to realize that the stages of progress, as we understand them, are not obligatory. Some of them may be skipped.

So it is with industry, and the conditions of life induced by industrial machinery, much of it may be skipped. And it is the continuous existence of an order like the Indian village community, which, when brought into relation with Western progress, seems to prove this. We in the West have passed through the condition of the Aryan village community. The conditions Dr. Coomaraswamy describes in India and Ceylon are very similar to the conditions that prevailed in mediæval England, Germany and France; they did not seem nearly so strange to Knox, writing in Stuart times, as they do to us. The 500 years that have passed between our middle ages and the growth of the great cities of machine industry may have proved that the destruction of the Western village community was inevitable, but it has not proved that where the village community still exists it need necessarily be destroyed. Indeed, we are finding out in the West that if the village tradition were still living it could still be utilized; we are even seeking to set up something like it in its place. For the great city of mechanical industry has come to a point when its disintegration is inevitable. There are signs that the devolution has already begun, both in England and America. The cry of "back to the land," the plea for a "more reasonable life," the revival of the handicrafts, the education of hand and eye, the agricultural revival, the German "*ackerbau*," the English small holding, our technical schools, all these things are indications of a need for finding something, if not to take the place of the village community, at least to bring once again into life those direct, simple, human and out-of-door things of which mechanical industry has deprived our working population. These things are necessary to our life as a people, and we shall have to find them somehow. Dr. Coomaraswamy does well to show how they still exist in great measure in the East, and it may be that the East, in her wisdom, and with her profound conservative instinct, will not allow them to be destroyed. She has, as Sir Geo. Birdwood puts it, let the races and the peoples for 3,000 years come and pass by; she may have taken this from one and that from another, but the fundamental democratic order of her society has remained, and it appears improbable, on the face of it, that we

English shall materially change it when so many others before us have left it undisturbed.

Indeed, there seems to be no reason, on the face of it, why we should aspire to do so. Some change we are certainly bringing, and bringing unconsciously, but it is a curious and suggestive thought that the spiritual reawakening in England, which goes now by the name of the higher culture, now by the name of Socialism, which has been voiced in our time by Ruskin and Morris, which has expressed itself in movements like the arts and crafts, or is revealed in the inspired paintings of the Pre-Raphaelites, demands just such a condition as in India our commercialisation is destroying. The spiritual reawakening in the West is appealing for a social condition in which each man shall have not only an economic but a spiritual status in the society in which he lives, or as some of us would prefer to put it, he shall have a stable economic status in order that he may have a spiritual status as well.

It is such a condition that still exists in India, where society is organized, as Dr. Coomaraswamy shows, upon a basis of "personal responsibility and co-operation," instead of, as with us, upon a basis of contract and competition. Even if we admit that the change in the Aryan of the West from the one basis to the other has been necessary in order to produce the conditions of modern progress, the scientific results of our civilization, in short, the great ships, it may yet be that the spiritual re-awakening that is beginning to stir the dry bones of our Western materialism may yet leave the ancient East fundamentally unchanged, and bring us once again into some kindred condition through our contact with her.

In the profoundly interesting address of the English artists in 1878, which bore the names of Morris, Burne-Jones, Millais, Edwin Arnold, Walter Crane and others, there is an appeal to the Government on behalf of Indian Arts and Crafts against the effects of English commercialism upon the production of Indian craftsmanship.

"At a time," say the signatories, "when these productions are getting to be daily more and more valued in Europe, these sources are being dried up in Asia, and goods which ought to be common in the market are now becoming rare treasures for museums and the cabinets of rich men. This result seems to us the reverse of what commerce ought to aim at."

But has commerce any aim? Is it as yet more than a blind force? The experience of 30 years has shown that this appeal of the English artists might have been as eloquently made on behalf of English as of Indian craftsmanship. For, indeed, the appeal is less against English Governmental action than against the conditions imposed upon the world by the development of industrial machinery, directed by commercialism. Industrial machinery which is blindly displacing the purpose of hand and destroying the individuality of human production; and commercialism, which is setting up one standard only, the quantitative standard, the standard of saleability.

To compass the destruction of commercialism and regulate and delimit the province of industrial machinery for the benefit of mankind, is now the work of the Western reformer. The spiritual re-awakening with us is taking that shape.

It is probable that in this effort of the Western artists, workmen, and reformers for the reconstruction of society on a saner and more spiritual basis, the East can help us even more than we shall help the East. What would we not give in England for a little of that "workshop service" which Dr. Coomaraswamy describes, in place of our half-baked evening classes in County Council Schools? What, in our effort at the revival of handicrafts in the decaying country-side, for some of those "religious trade union villages" of which Sir George Birdwood speaks?

There has come over Western civilization, in the last 25 years, a green sickness, a disbelief, an unrest;

it is not despondency, for in the finer minds it takes the form of an intense spiritual hopefulness; but it takes the form also of a profound disbelief in the value of the material conditions of modern progress, a longing to sort the wheat from the chaff, the serviceable from the useless, a desire to turn from mechanical industry and its wastefulness, and to look once more to the human hand, to be once again with Mother Earth.

"It behoves us," said Heraclitus, in the time of the beginnings of Hellenic civilization, "it behoves us to follow the common reason of the world; yet, though there is a common reason in the world, the majority live as though they possessed a wisdom peculiar each unto himself alone." This is so profoundly modern that it might almost be a comment upon English or American industrialism, did we not know that it applied equally to the peculiar intellectual individualism of Hellas, which disintegrated and destroyed her culture. But the "common reason of the world," if the words of Heraclitus are to be taken at their face value, includes the reason of the East, and with it the social order that has stood there unshaken for 3,000 years, and hence stood there long before the days of Heraclitus himself.

For our immediate purpose, too, the purpose of this book, the "common reason of the world" includes and defines the Indian craftsman and the Indian village community; it gives them a definite and necessary place not only in the Indian order of things, not only in the culture of the East, but in the world. It shows them to be reasonable and right, and it shows them, what is still more important, to be the counterpart one of the other.

Here once more we are learning from the East. The English craftsman and the English village are passing, or have passed away; and it is only in quite recent times that we have discovered that they, too, are the counterpart one of the other. Industrial machinery, blindly misdirected, has destroyed them both, and recent English land legislation has been trying, with allotment and small-holdings acts, to re-establish the broken village life. Those of us, however, that have studied the Arts and Crafts in their town and country conditions, are convinced that the Small Holding Problem is possible of solution only by some system of co-operation, and if some forms of craftsmanship are simultaneously revived and added to it. "Speak to the earth and it shall teach thee"; that is an old lesson, and it is true not only of England, but of all Western countries that have been touched by the green-sickness of industrial machinery. With us in the

West it is the newest of new ideas that the arts and crafts and the revival of agriculture are the corollary of one another. In India they always appear to have thought this, and to have held by the truth.

I never heard of the god Viśvakarma, the god of the Arts and Crafts, before I learned of him from Dr. Coomaraswamy. But he seems strangely like a personification of that Platonic idea of abstract beauty which for so many centuries has haunted the Western mind. Whether it be Plato or Plotinus, Pico della Mirandola or Rossetti, ever and again in the great periods of our Western development the idea recurs. Who knows, perhaps Viśvakarma is the god for whom we in the West, in our spiritual reawakening, are in search; possibly he can help us!

C. R. ASHBEE.

"The hand of a craftsman engaged in
his craft is always pure."—*Manu.*

"Those that are craftsmen of the people are
welcome over all the wide earth."—*Odyssey.*

"All these trust to their hands:
And everyone is wise in his work.
Without these cannot a city be inhabited."—*Ecclesiasticus.*

# CHAPTER I.

## THE VILLAGE CRAFTSMAN.

INDIAN society presents to us no more fascinating picture than that of the craftsman as an organic element in the national life. Broadly speaking, he is associated with that life in one of three ways: as a member of a village community; as a member of a guild of merchant craftsmen in a great city; or as the feudal servant of the king, or chieftain of a temple. First let us enquire into the position of the lesser craftsmen, within the agricultural village community.

The craftsmen thus working within the village community, are there in virtue of a perpetual contract whereby their services are given to the husbandmen, from whom they receive in return certain privileges and payments in kind. Each has his own duties to perform.

The woodwork of ploughs and other implements is made and repaired by the carpenter, the cultivator merely supplying the wood; the blacksmith supplies all the iron parts of the implements, and repairs them when necessary, the cultivator supplying the iron and charcoal, and working the bellows; and the potter* supplies each cultivator with the earthenware he needs. The list of artisans is not always the same, only those most indispensable to the community being found in all cases, such as the carpenter and blacksmith, potter and washerman. Others may be the barber-surgeon, messenger and scavenger, astrologer, or dancing girl. It will be seen that not all of these are technically craftsmen, but all occupy their position in virtue of the professional service which they render to the agricultural community. This is well illustrated by a verse of a fifteenth century Sinhalese poem† dealing with the origin of caste as a method of division of labour. The verse in question emphasizes the indispensable character of the services of the carpenter, tailor, washerman, barber and leather-worker.

"Both for the weddings and funerals of Rājas, Brāhmans, cultivators, merchants, S'ūdras and all men—the carpenter giving chairs, bedsteads, pavilions and the like—the tailor sewing and giving jackets and hats—the washer spreading awnings and bringing clean clothes—the barber cutting the hair and beard, trimming the face and adorning it

* *See Appendix* I.

† *Janavamsaya, trans. by H. Nevill, Taprobanian, Vol. I.*, 1886, *pp.* 74–93 *and* 103–114.

—the leather-worker stitching leather for the feet; thus these five are needed (alike) for the wedding and the funeral."

They are, indeed, in Ceylon, often spoken of as "the five servants."

It is mentioned in the *Mahavamsa* that the heads of the five trades were chosen as messengers to carry a welcome from Kitti Sirimegha to his son Parākrama, afterwards Parākrama Bāhu the Great. We thus catch a glimpse of the social status and importance of the "five trades," but it is not quite clear whether these are the five just referred to, or the five sections of the artificers proper—probably the former.

In Maratha villages, the craftsmen and menial servants formed a guild or institution, regulating the customary duties and remuneration of the craftsmen and servants, and called *bara balute* in as much as the full number of persons composing this body was reckoned at twelve. They included the craftsmen; the inferior servants, of low caste, as barbers and scavengers; and the *Bhat*, or village priest. They were all headed by the carpenter, who is called the *Patel* of the artizans, and decided all their disputes.*

* *"The system has, indeed, been a good deal broken up in British districts, where work by contract and competition has superseded customary service. But*

The presence of the craftsmen in the midst of a simple agricultural society made possible the self-contained life of the community, so striking a feature of the Indian village.

Living in a society organised on the basis of personal relations and duties,* which descended in each family from generation to generation, instead of belonging to a society founded on contract and competition, their payment was provided for in various ways, of which money payment was the least important and most unusual. The amount of money in circulation in the villages was, indeed, almost negligible, barter and personal service taking

---

*in the native States, where the innovating forces are less strong, the institution still flourishes, to the great satisfaction of all concerned."—"The Indian Raiyat as a Member of the Village Community," by Sir W. Wedderburn, London,* 1883.

* *Interesting light on village self-government is obtainable from the series of Chola inscriptions (ca.* 900–940 A.D.) *from the village of Ukkal, near Conjeevaram. The village was governed by an assembly (sabha or mahasabha), sub-divided into several committees. These were "the great men elected for the year," "the great men in charge of the tank," and "those in charge of gardens." The transactions of the assembly were put in writing by an officer who had the title of arbitrator (madhyastha), and who is also in one case called "accountant" (karanattan).—Hultzsch, South Indian Inscriptions, Vol. XXIX, pp.* 3, 28, *etc.*

the place of money payments. Wealth was hoarded if at all, rather in the form of jewellery than of money. Prosperity consisted in having several years' provisions of grain in one's granary. Anything of the nature of a shop or store was unknown.

The payment of craftsmen was either a payment in kind, or a grant of land, besides perquisites on special occasions. For their customary services, the craftsmen were repaid at harvest-time, receiving a fixed proportion of sheaves of grain from the crop collected on the threshing floor, or they might be given a share of the communal land. In the last case, it followed that every man was a cultivator and directly dependent on the land for his subsistence whether he were a husbandman, a goldsmith, or a washerman by caste. To take, at random, a few examples of these payments: In the Gujrah district of the Punjab, the village servants are paid by grain fees, so many bundles of the crop of wheat or barley, each bundle of such a size as may be tied by a string of three straws in length. In the villages of another province (N. W. P.) the following persons received each a share of grain for each "plough" of cultivated land in the village: the barber, washerman, carpenter, blacksmith and cowherd, besides a further allowance as an extra "when the business of the threshing-floor was over."* Thus, in

* *Baden-Powell, "Indian Village Community," p.17.*

Munda villages, "the *lohar*, or blacksmith, gets one *kat* of paddy and three *karais* for every plough in the village, and is also paid two or three *annas* for every new *phar* or plough-share; in a very few villages he holds half a *pawa* of land rent free."*

Almost always, too, there are set apart shares for religious and charitable purposes, before the remainder of the crop is divided between tenant and landlord, or removed by the tenant proprietor himself.† In Ceylon if a man wanted a new cloth he gave cotton from his clearing, and a present of grain to the weaver. Sometimes the craftsman was paid in this kind of way whenever his services were required, sometimes he received a perquisite only on special occasions; very much as in England the postman, employed by the community, receives an annual "Christmas box" from each individual at whose house he delivers letters. At New Year, for example, it was customary, in some parts of Ceylon, to tie up a coin in each garment sent to the wash; and the washerman had other perquisites beside; and so with the other servants and craftsmen of the village.

---

* *H. H. Risley, Census of India, Ethn. App., p.* 158.

† *Baden-Powell, loc. cit., p.* 17.

# CHAPTER II.

## THE CRAFT GUILDS OF THE GREAT CITIES.

"THE typical Hindu village consists exclusively of husbandmen; but as husbandry and manufacture cannot exist without each other, the village had to receive a number of artisans as members of its governing body. But they are all 'strangers within the gate,' who reside in a village solely for the convenience of the husbandmen on a sort of service contract. It is a perpetual contract, but in the lapse of 3,000 years, the artisans have constantly terminated their connection with a village, or have had to provide for sons in some other place, and they at once sought their livelihood in the towns which began to spring up everywhere round the centres of government, and of the foreign commerce of the country. It is in this way that the great polytechnical cities of India have been formed."

Let us pass on to a picture of the craftsman as a member of a great guild of merchant craftsmen, controllers of the wealth of mighty cities and once of the markets of the world.

"Community of interests would naturally draw together the skilled immigrants of these cities in trades unions; the bonds of which in India, as was also the case in ancient Egypt, are rendered practically indissoluble by the force of caste. . . . The trade guilds of the great polytechnical cities of India are not, however, always exactly coincident with the sectarian or ethnical caste of a particular caste of artisans. Sometimes the same trade is pursued by men of different castes, and its guild generally includes every member of the trade it represents without strict reference to caste. The government of the guilds or unions is analogous to that of the village communities and castes, that is, by hereditary officers. Each separate guild is managed by a court of aldermen or *mahajans*, literally 'great gentlemen.' Nominally it is composed of all the freemen of the caste, but a special position is allowed to the *seths*, lords, or chiefs of the guild, who are ordinarily two in number, and hold their position by hereditary right. The only other office-bearer is a salaried clerk or *gumasta*.

"Membership in the guild is also hereditary, but new-comers may be admitted into it on the payment of an entrance fee, which in Ahmedabad amounts to £2 for paper-makers, and £50 for tinsmiths. No unqualified person can remain in or enter a guild. It is not the practice to execute indentures of apprenticeship, but every boy born in a working caste of necessity learns his father's handicraft, and when he has mastered it, at once takes his place as an hereditary freeman of his caste or trade-guild; his father, or if he be an orphan, the young man himself, giving a dinner to the guild on the occasion. In large cities the guilds command great influence. The *Nagar-Seth*, or City Lord of Ahmedabad, is the titular head of all the guilds, and the highest personage in the city, and is treated as its representative by the Government. In ordinary times he does not interfere in the internal affairs of the guilds, their management being left to the chief alderman of each separate guild, called the *Chautano-Seth*, or 'lord of the market.' . . .The funds of the guilds of Western India, where they prevail chiefly among the Vaishnavas and Jainas of Gujarat, are for the greater part spent on charities, and particularly charitable hospitals for sick and helpless domestic animals: and in part also on the temples of the Maharajas of the Wallabhacharya sect of Vaishnavas, and on guild feasts. A favourite device for raising money is for the men of a craft or trade to agree on a certain day to shut all their shops but one. The right to keep open this one is then put up to auction, and the amount bid goes to the guild fund."*

The guilds likewise regulated the hours of labour, and the amount of work to be done in their

* *Sir George Birdwood*, "*Industrial Arts of India*," 1880, *pp.* 137–140.

workshops, by strict bye-laws, enforced by the levy of fines. But this old order is passing away.

"Under British rule, which secures the freest exercise of individual energy and initiative, the authority of the trade-guilds in India has necessarily been relaxed, to the marked detriment of those handicrafts, the perfection of which depends on hereditary processes and skill. The overwhelming importations of British manufactures also is even more detrimental to their prosperity and influence, for it has in many places brought wholesale ruin on the hereditary native craftsmen, and forced them into agriculture and even domestic service. But the guilds, by the stubborn resistance, further stimulated by caste prejudice, which they oppose to all innovations, still continue, in this forlorn way, to serve a beneficial end, in maintaining, for probably another generation, the traditional excellence of the sumptuary arts of India against the fierce and merciless competition of the English manufacturers. The guilds are condemned by many for fixing the hours of labour and the amount to be done in them by strict bye-laws, the slightest infringement of which is punished by severe fines, which are the chief source of their income. But the object of these rules is to give the weak and unfortunate the same chance in life as others more favoured by nature. These rules naturally follow from the theocratic conceptions which have governed the whole organisation of social life in India, and it is incontrovertible that the unrestricted development of the competitive impulse in modern life, particularly in the pursuit of personal gain, is absolutely antagonistic to the growth of the sentiment of humanity and of real religious convictions among men."*

The principles upon which they acted were, indeed, altogether socialistic, and realised as an accomplished fact many of the ideals for which the European worker is still fighting. Thus the guild both prevented undue competition amongst its members, and negotiated with other guilds in case of dispute amongst the craftsmen.

"In 1873, for example, a number of the bricklayers in Ahmedabad could not find work. Men of this class sometimes added to their daily wages by rising very early in the morning, and working overtime. But when several families complained that they could not get employment, the bricklayers' guild met, and decided that as there was not enough work for all, no member should be allowed to work in extra hours.† . . . The trade-guild or caste

---

* *Sir George Birdwood, loc. cit., p.* 139.

† *No incident could better illustrate the close relation of the industrial problems here treated of, and those in the modern West. For at the "Right to*

allows none of its members to starve. It thus acts as a mutual assurance society and takes the place of a poor law in India. The severest social penalty which can be inflicted upon a Hindu is to be put out of his caste."*

The following abbreviated details of the organisation of the Guilds in Ahmadābād are taken from the *Imperial Gazetteer of India, Vol. V., p.* 101 :

" In consequence of the importance of its manufactures of silk and cotton, the system of caste or trade unions is more fully developed in Ahmedābād than in any other part of Gujarāt. Each of the different castes of traders, manufacturers and artisans forms its own trade guild, to which all heads of households belong. Every member has a right to vote, and decisions are passed by a majority. In cases where one industry has many distinct branches, there are several guilds. Thus among potters, the workers of bricks, of tiles, and of earthen jars, are for trade purposes distinct; and in the great weaving trade, those who prepare the different articles of silk and cotton, form distinct

---

*Work" Conference at the Guildhall, of December,* 1908, *one of the resolutions passed and afterwards laid before the Prime Minister, included a condemnation of overtime, based on the very sound principle laid down above.*

* *Sir W. W. Hunter,* "*Brief History of the Indian Peoples,*" 1903, *ed. p.* 98.

associations. The objects of the guilds are to regulate competition among the members, *e.g.*, by prescribing days or hours during which work shall not be done. The decisions of the guilds are enforced by fines. If the offender refuses to pay, and all members of the guild belong to one caste, the offender is put out of caste. If the guild contains men of different castes, the guild uses its influence with other guilds to prevent the recusant member from getting work. Besides the amount received from fines, the different guilds draw an income by levying fees on any person beginning to practise his craft. This custom prevails in the cloth and other industries, but no fee is paid by potters, carpenters and other inferior artisans. An exception is also made in the case of a son succeeding his father, when nothing has to be paid. In other cases the amount varies, in proportion to the importance of the trade, from Rs. 50 to Rs. 500. The revenue derived from these fees, and from fines, is expended in parts to the members of the guild, and in charity. Charitable institutions, or *sadavart*, where beggars are fed daily, are maintained in Ahmedābād at the expense of the trade guilds."

How long ago the craftsmen were organized into these great municipal guilds, is suggested by a well-known passage in the Rāmāyana, describing the procession of citizens who went out into the forest with Bharata in search of Rāma. The gem-cutters, potters, weavers, armourers, ivory-workers, "well-known goldsmiths," together with many others, the foremost merchants as well as the citizens of all classes went out to search for Rāma; such a procession as even in the nineteenth century, perhaps even to-day, might be drawn together in one of the great merchant cities of Western India.

Again, we read in the Harivamsa,* of the preparations made for the royal family and citizens of Mathura to witness the contest between Krishna and Bālarāma and the king's champions.

"The amphitheatre was filled by the citizens, anxious to behold the games. The place of assembly was supported by octagonal painted pillars, fitted up with terraces, and doors, and bolts, with windows, circular or crescent-shaped, and accommodated with seats with cushions,"

and so on; and then we are told that

"The pavilions of the different companies and corporations, vast as mountains, were decorated with banners, bearing upon them the implements and emblems of the several crafts."

It is interesting to note also how much all this splendour depended upon these very crafts whose

---

* *Quoted by Wilson, Vishnu Purana, Vol. V., p.* 27.

position was thus recognized and honoured; for the tale goes on to say that

"The chambers of the inhabitants of the inner apartments shone near at hand, bright with gold, and painting, and net-work of gems; they were richly decorated with precious stones, were enclosed below with costly hangings, and ornamented above with spires and banners."

Compare with this, also, such a description as the following account of the preparations for the marriage of a princess (in the seventh century, A.D.): "From every county were summoned companies of skilled artists . . . Carpenters, presented with white flowers, unguents, and clothes, planned out the marriage altar. Workmen mounted on ladders, with brushes upheld in their hands and pails of plaster on their shoulders, whitened the top of the street wall of the palace. . . . The outer terraces resounded with the din of gold-workers engaged in hammering gold. Plasterers were beplastered with showers of sand which fell over them from freshly erected walls. A group of skilled painters painted auspicious scenes. Multitudes of modellers moulded clay figures of fishes, tortoises, crocodiles, cocoanuts, plantains and betel trees. Even kings girt up their loins and busied themselves in carrying out decorative work set as tasks by their sovereign." *

Another interesting mention of craftsmen in procession is found in the *Mahavamsa*, where we are told that following the officials in the annual Perahera at Kandy, were "people of strange countries, and men skilled in divers tongues, and numerous artificers and handicraftsmen." The period spoken of is the latter part of the eighteenth century.

I have not been able to hear of any accounts of guilds in Persia, where they must have existed from the earliest times. It is reported, however, that when in the recent troubles 14,000 people in Teheran took refuge in the foreign legations, each guild organised with perfect ease and order the policeing and feeding of its own people. This makes one realise how powerful an element in social stability is represented by the guilds even at the present day.

The nature of *guild responsibility*† is well indicated in some of the Tanjore inscriptions. A common form of pious offering consisted in the dedication of a lamp, *i.e.*, providing for a lamp to be kept continually burning before a certain image. This

---

* *Bana's 'Harsha Carita,' Trans. by E. B. Cowell and F. W. Thomas, p.* 124.

† *See also Appendix VII*

was generally arranged by the payment of a sum of money, or more often by the gift of a certain number of sheep or cattle to the guild of shepherds, who undertook to provide the necessary oil *in perpetuo*. The payment for thus maintaining one sacred lamp was 96 ewes, or 48 cows, or 16 she-buffaloes. "The shepherds who received the cattle, themselves and their people, viz., their relations, and the relations of the latter, had to supply *ghi* to the treasury of the Lord, as long as the sun and moon endure, at the daily rate of one *urakku* of *ghi* . . for each sacred lamp."*

The manner in which the shepherds as a guild bound themselves jointly as security for an individual contractor is as characteristic of true guild methods as their solidarity in the defence of their own interests would have been. In an inscription of Rajendra Soladeva at Tanjore, we have a detailed account of this acceptance of responsibility by the guild of shepherds: "We," runs the inscription, "all the following shepherds of this village . . . . agreed to become security for Eran Sattan, a shepherd of this village, (who) had received 90 ewes of this temple in order to supply *ghi* for burning one perpetual lamp. We shall cause the shepherd E.S. to supply daily to one perpetual lamp one *ulakku* of *ghi* . . . If he dies,

* *Hultzsch, South Indian Inscriptions, Vol. II., part III., p.* 251.

absconds, or gets into prison, fetters (or) chains, we all these aforesaid persons, are bound to supply *ghi* for burning the holy lamp as long as the sun and moon endure." This inscription ends with the name of a local merchant, who may have been the donor of the lamp.

The origin of the guild has not yet been worked out in any detail. With regard to the existence of actual guilds in early Buddhist times, the Jātakas give us but little information. The craftsmen associated in villages no doubt had their own laws and customs, tantamount to guild regulations, but of guilds in the great cities we hear little. In the *Nigrodha Jataka*, however, it is stated that to the king's treasurer was given also the judgeship of "all the guilds" (*sabbaseninam*). "Before that," says the Jātaka, "no such office existed, but there was this office ever after." In the *Uraga Jataka*, a guild quarrel (*senibhandana*) is mentioned, between two men in the king's service, who were heads of guilds (*seni-pamukha*).* Such evidence belongs, however, to the period of redaction of the Jātakas rather than to the times described in them. There can be no doubt, however, that at least the germ of the guild system existed at a very early time in the form of co-operative associations within the

* *But in Rouse's translation of this Jataka, the quarrel is between two soldiers, not guild masters.*

merchant community.* The merchant (*setthi*) himself was at a very early time a man of much wealth and social importance. He was the principal representative of the householder (*grahapati*) class, the typical burgher in the great town. The word *setthi* in some cases seems to imply a private trader, in others, a representative of commerce, holding an official position at court.† Many such merchants were evidently exceedingly wealthy; of one we are told that goods were brought to him in a caravan of no less than 500 wagons. But any detailed enquiry into the position of the trader, as a middleman, and not himself a craftsman, would be exceeding the limits of the subject of the present volume.

In slightly later literature the existence of guilds is more clearly indicated. In the Dharma sūtras it is stated that the farmers, merchants, cowherds and money-lenders had bye-laws of their own. applicable to their communities, and having due legal validity. In later law books, guilds (*sreni*) are often mentioned, *e.g.*, Manu, viii. 41, where it is stated that the king must examine and establish the laws of the guilds. Likewise in the epics, the guilds are recognised as an important factor in industrial and political life.†

---

* *Fick, "Indien zu Buddha's Zeit," pp.* 172–177.
† *Fick, loc. cit., p.* 172.

# CHAPTER III.

## THE FEUDAL CRAFTSMAN IN INDIA AND CEYLON.

LET us turn to look at the Indian craftsman as the feudal servant of the king, a baron, or of a religious foundation. In the so-called dark ages of the East and of the West, the patronage of art and craft by kings was a matter of course, and no court was complete, lacking the state craftsmen. He would have seemed a strange king who knew nought of art and craft, and cared less. Even Alfred the Great, amidst all the cares of protecting his troubled land, found time to care for craftsmanship and craftsmen, especially goldsmiths, and we are all familiar with the Alfred jewel that bears the legend, "Alfred had me made"; and this interest in jewellery reminds us of the Eastern proverb, that asks "who but the Rāja and the goldsmith should know the value of the jewel?" Still earlier evidence of the traditional royal interest in craft in the West may be gathered from such books as the "Mabinogion." When Kilhwch rode to Arthur's hall and sought admittance, "I will not open," said the porter. "Wherefore not?" asked Kilhwch. "The knife is in the meat, and the drink is in the horn," said the porter, "and there is revelry in Arthur's hall, and none may enter therein but the son of a king of a privileged country, or a craftsman bringing his craft."

So, too, in ancient Ireland we find it said to a similar applicant at the king's door, " no one without an art comes into Tara."*

Still later on, in the dark ages, we find, as one may learn from Professor Lethaby's " Westminster Abbey and the King's Craftsmen," that the royal masons, carpenters, smiths and painters were attached to the palace as much as a matter of course as the chief butler and cook, and that under the chief master-mason or carpenter a body of skilled journeymen was permanently engaged. We are wiser now, of course, and know that only the chief butler and cook are essential to the royal dignity; the craftsmen have gone, and only the butler, the cook and the clerk remain. Perhaps it is only worldly wisdom after all.

The royal craftsman in the East, however, is our immediate interest, and to him we must return.

We find him well established at a very early date. In the reign of Asoka (275-231 B.C.),

" Artisans were regarded as being in a special manner devoted to the royal service, and capital punishment was inflicted on any person who

* *In " Lugh of the Long Hand," version in Lady Gregory's " Gods and Fighting Men,"* 1904, *p.* 17.

impaired the efficiency of a craftsman by causing the loss of a hand or an eye. . . . Ship-builders and armour-makers were salaried public servants, and were not permitted, it is said, to work for any private person. The woodcutters, carpenters, blacksmiths and miners were subject to special supervision."*

Upon this subject of the regulation of the crafts I shall have more to say later.

Passing over a millenium and a half without endeavouring to trace the royal craftsman's footsteps one by one, we come to the time of the great Moghal Emperors in the North. From the Āīn-i-Akbari or Institutes of the Emperor Akbar, one of the three great rulers in whose mind the conception of a united India had taken shape, and one of the greatest rulers that the world has seen, we are told of the skilled Indian and foreign craftsmen maintained in the palaces of the Moghals.

Akbar had in his service many artists, to the end that they "might vie with each other in fame, and become eminent by their productions." Weekly he inspected the work of every artist, and gave due reward for special excellence. He also personally superintended the making of the weapons forged and decorated in the armoury. He was very fond of shawls, of which many kinds were made

* *Vincent Smith, "Early History of India," p.* 120.

in the palace, and classified according to date, value, colour and weight. He had also jewellers and damasceners, inlayers and enamellers, engravers and lapidaries, and craftsmen of all kinds. It is to be observed that all this did not represent in Akbar, any more than it did in Alfred, the mere luxury of an idle or weak monarch, but belonged to a definite conception of the kingly state and duty recognized by one of the greatest rulers the world has seen.

"His majesty taking great delight in, and having patronised this art from the commencement of his reign, has caused it to arrive at high perfection. With that view, this department was established, in order that a number of artists being collected together, might vie with each other for fame, and become eminent by their productions. Every week the daroghas and tepookchies bring to his majesty the performance of every artist, when, in proportion to their merits, they are honoured with premiums, and their salaries are increased."

"Through the attention of his majesty, a variety of new manufactures are established in this country; and the cloths fabricated in Persia, Europe and China have become cheap and plenty. The skill of the manufacturers has increased with their number, for his majesty has made himself acquainted with the theory and practice in every stage of the business, so as to be able to discover the merits of the workmen; thus by bringing the arts into credit, the natives are encouraged to give application, and they speedily gain a complete knowledge of their profession."

The Emperor Akbar took a personal delight in painting; he is reported to have said that—

"There are many that hate painting, but such men I dislike. It appears to me as if a painter had quite peculiar means of recognizing God, for in sketching anything that has life, and devising its limbs one after the other, he must feel that he cannot bestow a soul upon his work, and is forced to think of God, the only giver of life, and will thus increase his knowledge."

No wonder that the crafts flourished under such conditions; and it is very certain that Musalmān puritanism did not, as a matter of fact, injure Indian art in the way that the contact with Western civilization has injured it. Just as in England the churches have suffered more from churchwardens than from puritans, so Indian art has suffered more from philistines—of the Macaulay type—than from iconoclasts.

The thing which perhaps most interests us from the craftsman's point of view is the security and hereditary character of his position. Sir John Chardin tells us of the Persian kings in the seventeenth century that they

"entertain a large number of excellent master-workmen, who have a salary and daily rations for all their lives, and are provided with all the materials for their work. They receive a present and an increase of salary for every fine work they produce."

Sir George Birdwood says:

"In the East the princes and great nobles and wealthy gentry, who are the chief patrons of these grand fabrics, collect together in their own houses and palaces all who gain reputation for special skill in their manufacture. These men receive a fixed salary and daily rations, and are so little hurried in their work that they have plenty of time to execute private orders also. Their salaries are continued even when through age or accident they are past work; and on their death they pass to their sons, should they have become skilled in their father's art. Upon the completion of any extraordinary work it is submitted to the patron, and some honour is at once conferred on the artist, and his salary increased. It is under such conditions that the best art work of the East has always been produced."

There is, for example, in the India Museum an engraved jade bowl, on which a family in the employ of the Emperors of Delhi was engaged for three generations. In these days when churches are built by contract and finished to the day or week, it is difficult to realise the leisurely methods of the older craftsmen. Do not mistake leisure for laziness;

they are totally and entirely different things. The quality of *leisure* in old work is one of its greatest charms, and is almost essential in a work of art. Haste and haggling have now almost destroyed the possibility of art, and until they are again eliminated from the craftsman's work it will not be possible to have again such work as he once gave to his fellows. In other words, society must either decide to do without art, as it mostly does decide at the present day, or else it must make up its mind to pay for art and endow its craftsmen. You cannot both have art and exploit it.

The royal appreciation of art and craft in the East at various times is further illustrated by the existence of kings who themselves practised a craft. I have collected two or three of these instances, but have no doubt that many more could be found by searching the pages of Indian history.

In the Kusa Jātaka, it is recorded that Prince Kusa, not wishing to marry, conceived the idea of having a beautiful golden image made, and of promising to marry when a woman of equal beauty should be found. He summoned the chief smith, and giving him a quantity of gold, told him to go and make the image of a woman. In the meanwhile he himself took more gold, and fashioned it into the image of a beautiful woman, and this image he had robed in linen and set in the royal chamber. When the goldsmith brought his image, the prince found fault with it, and sent him to fetch the image placed in the royal chamber. At first mistaking this image for a daughter of the gods, he feared to touch it; but being sent to fetch it a second time, he brought it; it was placed in a car and sent to the Queen Mother with the message, "When I find a woman like this, I will take her to wife."

This story is no doubt legendary, but shows at least that at the time of its composition the practise of a craft was not considered derogatory to the honour of a prince. A more historical mention of a royal craftsman is the reference to King Jetthatissa of Ceylon, in the *Mahavamsa*. "He was," says this chronicle, "a skilful carver. This monarch, having carried out several arduous undertakings in painting and carving, himself taught the art to many of his subjects. He sculptured a beautiful image of the Bodhisatta so perfect that it seemed as if it had been wrought by supernatural power; and also a throne, a parasol and a state room with beautiful work in ivory made for it."

For other instances of royal craftsmanship, we may turn to the Arabian literature. Sir Richard Burton, speaking of the conversation between the fisherman and the Caliph in the tale of Nur-al-din Ali and the Damsel al-Jalis, says:

"Most characteristic is this familiarity between

the greatest man then in the world and his pauper subject. The fisherman alludes to a practice of Al-Islam, instituted by Caliph Omar, that all rulers should work at some handicraft in order to spare the public treasure. Hence Sultan Mu'Ayyad of Cairo was a calligrapher who sold his handwriting, and his example was followed by the Turkish Sultans Mahmud, Abd-al-Majid and Abd-al-Aziz."*

Another royal craftsman is spoken of in "The Three Princes of China"†; the Shaykh's independent point of view is especially noteworthy. The tale is not, of course, historical, but reflects an idea which evidently appeared quite reasonable to the audience.

A certain Sultan fell in love with a Badaw girl who was standing with the Shaykh her father considering his retinue. After returning to his palace, the Sultan sent for her father, and asked the girl in marriage. The Shaykh, however, answered: "O, our Lord the Sultan, I will not give up my daughter save to one who hath a handicraft of his own, for verily trade is a defence against poverty, and folk say:—Handicraft an it enrich not still it veileth (poverty)." The Sultan remonstrated: "O, man, I am Sovran and Sultan, and with me

---

* "*Arabian Nights,*" *Vol. II.*
† *Burton, Supplemental Nights, V. 222.*

is abundant good"; but the Shaykh replied, "O, king of the age, in king-craft there is no trust." Whereat the Sultan "presently summoned the Shaykh of the mat-makers and learnt from him the craft of plaiting, and he wove these articles of various colours, both plain and striped."

So much for princely craftsmen in the East.

One extract from the Sinhalese chronicles will show how real could be the royal appreciation of the arts and crafts; it is a message from Vijaya Bāhu to his father, Parākrama Bāhu II., who reigned in the thirteenth century. It relates to the rebuilding of a city that had been laid waste by foreign enemies, and subsequently abandoned altogether. "There are now," runs the message, "in the city of Pulatthi, palaces, image-houses, viharas, parivenas, cetiyas, relic-houses, ramparts, towers, bird-shaped houses, mansions, open halls, preaching halls, temples of the gods, and the like buildings, whereof some are yet standing, although the trees of the forest have grown over and covered them. Others thereof are fast falling, because that the pillars thereof are rotten and cannot support them. Others, alas! are bent down with the weight of huge walls split from top to bottom, and are tumbling down because that there is nothing to bear them up. Sad, indeed, is it also to see others, unable to stand by reason of decay and weakness, bending down to their fall day by day, like unto old men. Some there are with broken ridge poles and damaged beam ends, and some with roofs fallen down and the tiles thereof broken. In some the tiles have slipped through the breaches of the decayed roof, and in others only the walls and pillars remain. Some there are with fallen doors, and doorposts that have been displaced, and others with loose staircases and ruined galleries. Of some buildings there only remain the signs of their foundations, and in others even the sites cannot be distinguished. What need is there of further description? This city, which is now so ugly and displeasing to the eye, we purpose to make beautiful and pleasant. Let the king grant us leave thereto, and let the feast of coronation be held in the great city afterwards." And so, as the chronicle tells us, he did indeed; for "he gathered together smelters, turners, basket makers, blacksmiths, potters, goldsmiths, painters, porters, labourers, slaves, outcastes, skilful bricklayers, masons, carpenters, and divers workers in stone. And, further he assembled all sorts of blacksmiths' tools, such as bellows, sledge-hammers, pincers, and anvils; and also numerous sharp saws, adzes, axes, wood-cleavers, stone-cutters' chisels, knives, hammers, spades, mats, baskets, and the like;

all these . . . did he send unto his royal son."*

Let us examine in slightly greater detail the organisation of the king's craftsmen, that is the State craftsmen, in Ceylon, as it existed up to the day on which the British Governor replaced the Kandyan king. It must be first understood that the organisation of society was altogether feudal. The possession of land was the foundation of the king's right to the services and contributions of the people, and *vice versa*. For all land held, service was due from the tenant to the king, that is to the State. The lands and services were inseparably associated, and as a rule descended from father to son in the same family, and this remained the same even when the services were bestowed by the king on individuals or given to religious foundations. There was thus no free trade in land; and every man had his place in the society, and his work. Landholders were classed in accordance with the services due from them. The vast majority were cultivators, whose duty it was to keep the State granaries well supplied; others were the soldiers, the musicians, the washermen, the servants, the potters, and weavers, and the craftsmen proper, viz.: the carpenters, gold-

---

* *Mahavamsa, Ch. LXXXVIII.*

smiths, masons, ivory carvers, armourers, founders and painters, altogether perhaps a tenth of the population. All of these owned service to the king in respect of the lands they held. The lands descended in the family from generation to generation, and were cultivated by the owners. Everyone was thus directly dependent on the land for his living. The craftsmen, however, were not serfs, nor *adscriptus glebæ*, as a tenant had always the right to refuse service and surrender his land. This, however, only happened in rare instances, as during the last king's reign, when too arduous services were sometimes required. Of temple tenants, Knox remarked that their duties in this life were so easy, that they might expect to suffer for it in the next! But hereditary social status and landholding went very much together, and to surrender the family service land would have been the last thing desired by a Kandyan craftsman. If, by chance, the succession failed, this would be remedied by adoption of a pupil and heir of the same caste.

The State Craftsmen fell into two groups, those of the "Four Workshops" (*Pattal Hatara*), who worked always at the palace, and those of the separate districts, who had to do certain shares of work at the palace, but were more often at home, where they had to work for the local officials; and those of the artificers' department (*Kottal-badde*).

The best of the higher craftsmen, those of the "Four Workshops," formed a close, largely hereditary corporation, and the position was highly valued. From their number were chosen the foremen of the District Craftsmen (*Kottal-badde*). The four shops were known as the "Regalia," the "Crown," the "Golden Sword," and the "Lion Throne" workshops respectively; but the craftsmen seem to have passed from one to another according to the work required of them. These families were of considerable standing, often possessing very valuable landed property settled upon them by the king on the occasion of their first arrival from India, if, as was often the case, they were of Indian origin, or granted as a reward for subsequent services. The very name *galladda* (*gam-ladda*), by which the superior craftsmen are often designated, means one who possesses or holds a village. There are some families of craftsmen whose history can be traced from at least the fourteenth century by means of the original and subsequent grants which they received from the Sinhalese kings. I give an example of one of these grants, dated 1665 A.D.:

"During the reign of His Majesty the mighty Emperor Rāja Simha, . . . as Marukona Ratna Ābharana Vedakārayā reported himself at the palace, orders were given to make certain pieces of jewellery required for the royal dress; and when he had made and submitted these pieces of jewellery to the great king, he stated that he needed the Mottuvela Nila-panguve Badavedilla in Pallesiya Pattuva of Asgiri Kōrale, in the Disāvanaya of Mātale for his maintenance . . . and His Majesty . . . did . . . in the year of Saka, 1587, absolutely grant the high and low lands in Mottuvela Badavedilla . . . to Marukona Ratna Ābharana Vedakārayā, to be possessed without any disturbance or hindrance during the existence of the Sun, the Moon, Kandy and the Mahāveli river."

As another instance of a special grant may be cited the following charter held by a Kandyan craftsman:

"When the king of kings, Srī Sanghabō Senasammata Vikrama Bāhu, was reigning in Senkadagala (Kandy), he ordered on a full moon day of the twentieth year of his reign, two sheets of cloth, twenty cubits by nine cubits, to be woven, and caused Ācharilla Dityaya and his son Sivanta Dityaya to paint thereon the likeness of Buddha seated on a Vajrāsana and surrounded by Sakra, Brahma, and other Devas. On the completion of painting the two sheets, he ordered the ceremony of placing pots full of water, and of other rites; and on the completion of the Nētra Pinkama, his hands having been washed [ceremonial purification after painting the eyes of the image, performed by the king himself, as here, or by a craftsman in royal costume], he was graciously pleased to bestow on the two artists, with the object of satisfying them and to enable them to make offerings to Buddha, fields to the extent of four *amunu*, together with the high land and trees thereon, as well as the houses and all other things pertaining thereto . . . to be held absolutely from generation to generation.

"Now know all ye that are concerned, that the said properties having been bestowed under royal assent to be enjoyed by these artists, their sons, grandsons, and their subsequent generations: if any king, sub-king, courtier, minister, or whatsoever person were to dispute the right to this *badavedilla* [land given to a craftsman for his subsidence], such person or persons shall be born in the eight hills successively. . . .But, on the other hand, if any person shall confirm and uphold the said gift, he shall after death be born successively in the six heavens . . . and after the termination of the enjoyments of the bliss of these heavens, shall be born in the kingdom of Ketumati, where he shall see Maitri Buddha, by whom the law shall be preached to him, whose holy priesthood he shall enter into, arahatship, and subsequently Nirvāna.

"In this tenor the royal decree was issued, and

by command this copperplate Sannas was inscribed by me, Sanhassivanta Nainarumbha. By the merit acquired inscribing this, may I be born in the age of Maitri Buddha."

Besides such grants of land, the king used to reward individual craftsmen with gifts of cloth, money, etc., and by the bestowal of honours and titles.

The District Craftsmen (*Kottal-badde*—lit. Artificers' Department—one of the Fourteen Departments of Public Works under the Kandyan kings) differed from those of the Four Workshops in not being liable to permanent service at the court. Some of them served in relays for periods of two months at a time, others worked only for the governors of districts, and not directly for the court. In certain of the districts the Governor (*Disava*) himself held the office of *Kottal-badde Nilame*, or Overseer of Craftsmen, and in this case he usually appointed from their number a *Kottal-badde* Vidāne, or officer acting as his lieutenant. In other districts, two Overseers of Craftsmen were appointed by the king. It is interesting that on one occasion, in the seventeenth century, a Dutchman was appointed Overseer of Craftsmen. He entered the king's service for the love of a Sinhalese woman, and was made "Courtalbad," "which is chief over all the smiths and carpenters in *Cande Uda*."*

The *Kottal-badde* craftsmen in one district consisted of the following:

I. Seven *vaduvo* who did carpenters' work for the king or governor; they were usually employed at the royal timber yard.

Five *liyana vaduvo*, or turners.

Five *sittaru*, or painters.

Fourteen *i-vaduvo*, or arrow-makers, who made bows, arrows, spears, staves, etc., and gauded them with lac; of these men, two worked in the royal armoury.

Fourteen *atapattu karayo*, who furnished or executed fine work, and were principally employed in ornamenting and inlaying locks, guns, knives, etc., with gold, silver, or brass; two of them worked in the royal armoury.

Four *badallu*, or silversmiths, workers in gold, silver, brass, or copper; two of them worked in the royal armoury.

One *gal-vaduva*, or mason.

---

* *Robert Knox*, "*An Historical Relation of the Island Ceilon*," 1682, *p.* 181.

Twenty *mul-acari*, or blacksmiths, a certain number of whom, varying according to the exigency of the service, attended constantly in Kandy, and erecting workshops near the Disāva's house, executed all kinds of common ironwork, for which the metal was furnished them.

Eight blacksmiths without regular service lands such as the foregoing held. These blacksmiths had to appear before the Disāva at New Year with a knife and scissors each, and were liable to be called on for work in any time of emergency.

Ten *Disava acari*, who worked for the Disāva only.

Twenty-two potters, in two divisions, under the orders of officers of the same caste appointed by the Disāva. The two divisions undertook turns of duty of one month each in rotation with the potters of other districts, the turns recurring once in ten months. When at home in their own district, they had only to furnish earthenware for the Disāva, for the rest-houses, and for the king or ambassadors if they came to the district.

The following may serve as actual examples of individual craftsmen's tenure:

A goldsmith holding half an acre and owing service to the Gadalādeniya Dēvāle (temple) in Ceylon, had to supply a silver ring for the "festival tree," and repair the golden insignia for use at the *perahera* (annual festival and procession); put up and decorate booths on the same occasion; supply a measure of oil for the Kārti festival; and give annually to the two lay officers of the temple, two silver rings each. These services were commutable for Rs. 7.35 (nearly 10s.).

A blacksmith held land of the same extent, his services (commutable for Rs. 5.85) were to give iron utensils for the temple kitchen; work as a blacksmith; clean the palanquin and cressets for the *perahera*; nail laths; annually present a pair of scissors and an arecanut-slicer; clean the temple yard, and put up and decorate a booth; give a measure of oil for the Kārti festival; and at each of the four annual festivals to present the lay officers with an arecanut-slicer each.

It must be understood that materials (such as iron, charcoal, etc., for the smith, gold for the goldsmith, pigments for the painter), and food (and lodging) were in all such cases provided by the proprietor for the tenant when working away from home, whether at court, at the manor house, or at the temple.

The following is an example of a potter's tenure:

A tenant of the Talgahagoda Vihāra (Buddhist temple) held 4¼ acres of land. His services (commutable for Rs. 10.35) were to give at New Year one piece of pottery; for the ceremony of sprinkling milk, two pots; one yoke load of pottery on the 15th of the month of Bat; 63 Kārti lamps on the 15th of the month of Il; four pots and four dishes on the 15th of Durutta for the New Rice (Harvest Home) festival; 50 dishes once a year for the monastery; two vases and two jugs to each of the two vihāras; and to tile the two vihāras (when necessary).

For the most part, of course, there was no wage payment of the state craftsmen, for they were otherwise provided for under the admirable land system I have referred to; but in the case of the many religious buildings undertaken by the Sinhalese kings, it was otherwise, as the king in these cases always desired to remunerate the craftsmen himself directly, in order that the meritorious work might be his very own, and not anybody else's. Thus also we read of the builder King Duttha Gāmanī, in the second century B.C., that when setting about the building of a great monastery called the Brazen Palace, that

"The generous Rāja, at the very beginning of the undertaking, laid down eight hundred thousand pieces of money at each of the four gates, and announced that on this occasion it was unfitting to exact unpaid labour; setting, therefore, a value on the work performed, he paid in money."

Nearly all the later kings were builders, too, and it was in the building of Buddhist temples that the State craftsmen were chiefly occupied when the requirements of the court and the armoury had been met. And on all these occasions the craftsmen were liberally and specially rewarded. I wish I could give some adequate idea of the passion for religious building which possessed the Sinhalese kings, and of the way in which this stimulated the production of works of art and craft. Perhaps I shall best do this by quoting from a typical temple charter. At Degaldoruva, in the eighteenth century, the King's younger brother had a cave temple enlarged, and he "caused stone walls to be put up and doors and windows to be set with keys and bars, and an image of Buddha of twelve cubits in length to be made in a reclining posture, and six other images in a sitting posture to be placed at the head and feet of the image, and also caused twenty-four Buddha's images to be depicted on the ceiling and on the walls within and without, and other workmanship and paintings to be made thereon and upon the stone pillars, the roof of the front court to be put up with beams and rafters, and covered with tiles, and on the cross walls thereof a representation of hell and heaven. . . . and having furnished the temple with curtains, ceiling cloths, umbrellas, flags, drums, oboes, etc. . . . His Majesty . . .

ordered the ceremony of painting the eyes to be performed, and His Majesty also furnished all the necessaries thereto, and having granted much riches in clothes, money and other things to the artificers, the painters and the stone-cutters, His Majesty received merit and was filled with ecstacy."

One other extract is quoted from a *sannasa* or charter [Gangārāma Vihāra, Kandy]:

"Kīrti Srī Rāja Simha . . . caused a vihāra to be made containing stone walls of thirteen cubits in length, seven in breadth, and eleven in height, surrounded by stone pillars, and above a roof with rafters covered with tiles. Within the walls a stone image of nine cubits in height was made, its robes beautified with painting of vermilion, its different members covered with leaves of gold, painted about with the five colours, and completed after the enshrinement of bodily relics. . . . In the year of Saka, 1674 (A.D. 1752), of the month Poson, and on Monday, the eighth day of the increase of the moon, under the constellation Hata, eyes were affixed to the image, accompanied with great solemnity, rejoicings and excessive offerings, and the craftsmen were satisfied by appropriate gifts."*

* *A. C. Lawrie, "Gazetteer of the Central Province," p.* 817 *(with verbal alterations).*

The king, the nobles and the people, especially the craftsmen, were brought into intimate and even affectionate association on these occasions.

But not all of the craftsmen in Ceylon were servants of the king or the state directly. Every religious foundation of importance had its own lands, occupied by husbandmen and craftsmen, who owed service to the temple, just as the tenants of a royal manor owed service to the king. Let us examine a few instances of such tenancies. One of the goldsmith-tenants of the Daladā Māligāva, the great Buddhist temple in Kandy, for example, held three acres of land. For this his services, light enough, were to go to the temple and polish the gold and silver vessels and implements of the temple during six days in the year, and to give a nut-slicer and two silver rings to the lay-chief of the temple every New Year. When on duty at the temple, the tenant received his meal three times a day. The blacksmith tenant of another temple held half an acre, and owed somewhat harder service ; he was to give iron utensils for the kitchen, work as a blacksmith, clean the palanquins and lamps, nail laths, give a pair of scissors and a nut-slicer, clean the court-yard and put up booths for the annual festival, and give a measure of lamp oil for another annual celebration, and at each festival to present to the lay officials of the temple a nut-slicer each. So much, indeed, were the crafts bound up with the temples, so much occupied were the craftsmen, whether royal craftsmen or temple tenants, in either building, restoring or supplying the requirements of temples, that the art was really as distinctively religious as the Gothic art of the middle ages, and in the same way too, it was an art for, and understood by, the whole people.

Similar conditions probably prevailed from the earliest times. An interesting record of temple craftsmen is given in the tenth century inscription of Mahinda IV., at Mihintale, in Ceylon. The inscription describes the administration and organisation of a well-endowed* Buddhist monastery. The section treating of craftsmen runs as follows: "(There shall be granted) to the chief master-artisan all that belongs to the guild of artisans at Bond-vehera; to two master-artisans, to eight carvers, and to two bricklayers—to (all of) these, the village Vadu-devagama. To each of the two workers in wood (shall be assigned) one *kiriya* (of land); to each of the two master-lapidaries [or

* *Mahavamsa, Ch. L.*: "*And he* [*Sena I.*, 1389–1409 *A.D.*] *built, as it were by a miracle, a great vihara at Arittha-pabbala, and endowed it with great possessions, and dedicated it to the Pansakulika brethren. And he gave to it also royal privileges and honours, and a great number of keepers for the garden, and servants and artificers.*"

goldsmiths ?], three *kiriya* (of land) ; to each of the two blacksmiths, one *kiriya* (of land) ; to the lime-burners, the village Sunubol-devagama ; to the six cartmen, the village Dunumugama." Also, " to a painter, two *kiriya* (of land) " ; " to each of the five potters who supply daily five earthen pots, one *kiriya* (of land)."*

Again, in the Jētavanārāma Sanskrit inscription (first half of ninth century), relative to the administration of another Buddhist monastery, we read : "[There shall be] clever stone-cutters and skilful carpenters in the village devoted to the work of [temple] renewal. They all . . . shall be experts in their [respective] work. To each of them shall be given of one and a half *kiri* [in sowing extent] for their maintenance . . . an enclosed piece of ground. And one *hena* [or a plot of dry land] shall be granted to each of them for the purpose of sowing fine grain. Means of subsistence of the [same] extent [as is] given to one of these shall be granted to the officer who superintends work. Moreover, when thus conferring maintenance on the latter person, his work and so forth shall [just] be ascertained, and the name of him [thus] settled [with a livelihood], as well as his respective duties, shall be recorded in the register. Those of the five castes

---

* *Wickremasinghe*, "*Epigraphia Zeylanica*," *Vol. I.*, *p.p* 111, 112.

who work within the precincts of the monastery shall receive [their] work after it has been apportioned, and they alone shall be answerable for its excellence [lit. purity]. The limit [of time] for the completion of [a piece of] work [thus apportioned] is two months and five days. Blame [shall be attributed] to the superintendents, the vārikas, and the labourers who do not perform it according to arrangement. Those who do not avoid blame . . . shall be deprived of their share [of land]."

The craftsmen were provided with all materials, and probably fed while at work at the monastery, but received no wages in money; their means of subsistence being the portion of land allotted to each, and cultivated by other members of the family, and, probably, as at the present day, by themselves also in times of ploughing, sowing and harvest. The same conditions prevailed in mediæval England in this respect.* This relation between craft and agriculture is very important in view of the character of the modern social problems of the Western craftsman, alluded to in Mr. Ashbee's foreword.

---

* *See Thorold Roger's "Six Centuries of Work and Wages," pp.* 46, 179, 180. *To draw any detailed comparison with the social conditions in mediæval Europe would, however interesting, have been beyond the scope of the present volume.*

Some inscriptions of Rāja Rāja (A.D. 985–1018) at the great Tanjore (Tañjavūr) temple in Southern India, give interesting details of craftsmen attached to the temple, recalling the records of the establishment at Mihintale above referred to. One inscription refers to the produce of land assigned to temple servants before the 29th year of the king's reign. Besides the lands assigned to a large number of *devadasis* (400), there were:

"For one man belonging to the potters (*kusavar*) of the sacred kitchen, one share (of land), and for ten (other) men half a share each; altogether, to the potters of the high street of Sūrasikhāmani, six shares."

"To the jewel-stitcher . . . one and a half share."

"For one brazier (*kannan*), one share."

"For one master carpenter (*taccacarya*), one and a half share, and for two (other) men, one and a half share; altogether . . . three shares."

"For a person who performs the duty of superintending goldsmiths (*kankani tattan*), by selecting one man and letting him do the work, to . . . the superintending goldsmith of the minor treasures of the Lord Srī-Rāja(rājad)eva, one share."*

* *Hultzsch, "South Indian Inscriptions," Vol. II., part III., p.* 259.

(Also for two other carpenters, three-quarters of a share each; and for four tailors, one and a half share each, and for two other tailors, one share each).

But besides the royal and religious manors, and their tenants, craftsmen included, there were also manors in the possession of chieftains and officials, held by them either for life or office, or for ever; granted in the first instance for public service in peace or war. So it came about that just as there were craftsmen working always for the king at court, or bringing in to court the work done for the king at home, so at the local chieftain's manor-house were to be seen craftsmen working for him patiently and contentedly, receiving only their meals, while their families cultivated the lands for which service was due to the chief; and amongst the tenants of the chief's demesne, these craftsmen were by no means the least important or the least honoured.

I give one instance of such a tenant's holding and services. At Pāldeniya, in Ceylon, a tenant held land of something over an acre in extent; for this he had to pay eightpence annually as a fee; to appear twice a year and give a piece of silversmith's work worth 3s. 4d.; to work at the manor-house thirty days a year, being supplied with food and charcoal; to accompany the Lord of the Manor on important occasions twice a year.

## VILLAGES OF CRAFTSMEN.

The craftsmen in Ceylon were to a great extent associated in villages; that is to say, a whole village or manor would be sometimes entirely a village of craftsmen. In this we trace a survival of old conditions. In the Sūci Jātaka, for example, we get a picture of just such a village of craftsmen:

"The Bodhisatta was born in the kingdom of Kāsi, in a smith's family, and when he grew up became skilled in the craft. His parents were poor. Not far from their village was another smith's village of a thousand houses. The principal smith of the thousand was a favourite of the king, rich, and of great substance. . . . People came from the villages round to have razors, axes, ploughshares and goads made."*

In another Jātaka, the Alīnacitta Jātaka, we read that there was

"once upon a time a village of carpenters not far from the city, in which five hundred carpenters lived. They would go up the river in a vessel, and enter the forest, where they would shape beams and planks for house-building, and put together the frame-work of one-storey and two-storey houses, numbering all the pieces from the mainpost onwards; these then they brought down to the river bank, and put them all aboard; then rowing down stream

* "*The Jataka,*" *Ed. E. B. Cowell,* 1895-1908, *No.* 387.

again, they would build houses to order as it was required of them; after which, when they received their wage, they went back again for more materials for the building, and in this way they made their livelihood."†

The Pāli Jātakas supply us with a considerable amount of information regarding the position of craftsmen in early Buddhist times. The most striking features of the social organisation of the craftsmen at this time are: the association of craftsmen in villages, the hereditary character of the craft, and the importance of the Elder, or master-craftsman. These conditions, like so many other early Buddhist social features, have persisted in mediæval and even until modern times in Ceylon, where we find, for example, smiths' villages and potters' villages, where all or nearly all the inhabitants belong to one occupational caste. At the same time, it is important to distinguish the social significance of the craftsmen thus associated in villages, and that of the "village craftsman" proper, who is the sole representative of his calling, and is the endowed servant of an agricultural community. In the one case, the purchaser has to seek the maker of wares in his own home; in the other, the craftsman is himself permanently estab-

† *Loc. cit.*, *No.* 156. *For potters, see the Kumbhakara Jataka.*

lished amongst his patrons. In late mediæval Ceylon the two conditions existed side by side.

Besides the craftsmen thus organised in extra-urban communities of their own, we have, on the one hand, craftsmen and merchants (principally the latter) living in the city, in their own streets and quarters; and, on the other, craftsmen of no particular caste, or considered as belonging to despised castes. Thus, wheelwrights and carriage builders belonged to the inferior or lesser castes with which they are classified in the Suttavibhanga, together with the Candala, Nesada, and Pukkusa *castes* (lesser castes, *hinajati*), while the basket makers, potters, weavers, leather-workers and barbers are said to be of the lesser *trades* (*hina sippa*). The distinction in thought between caste and trade became much less clear in later times; in early Buddhist times caste was less defined and crystalised than it afterwards became, and there was no division of Sūdras so-called.

All workers in wood were comparatively low in social rank, the joiner, however, naturally much less so than the workers in cane, as is the case also at the present day in Ceylon. It should be observed that it was not handicraft itself that gave a low social rank to certain groups of craftsmen, but rather the fact that these groups consisted essentially of aboriginal non-Aryan races practising crafts that were known to them before the arrival of the Aryans (weaving, pottery, basket-making).

It would be a very great mistake, however, to suppose that the social status of the artist or craftsman was invariably low. This certainly cannot have been the case in the finest period of Indian art, when the national culture found expression at least as completely in art as in literature or music. As we have seen, the *kammalar* in Southern India claim a social status equal or superior to that of Brāhmans; and in Ceylon the position of the superior craftsmen, often the grantees of whole villages, and served by tenants and villeins of their own, was, though technically, and as regards the essential point of intermarriage inferior, in other ways considerably superior to that of the European craftsman at the present day. The skilful and noted craftsman was a person to be approached with gifts, and treated with respect on account of his skill and learning.

Just the same thing is indicated in that interesting episode related in the *Katha-kosa*, where a prince named Amaradatta is described as falling in love with a beautiful statue, and weeping and complaining to his friend Mitrānanda. "At this moment a native of the place, a merchant, Ratnasāgara by name, came into that temple. The merchant asked,

'Why are you two distracted by grief?' Mitrānanda told the merchant, though with difficulty, the case of Amaradatta. The merchant said to himself: 'Oh, the might of Cupid triumphs! There is in his mind a passion even for a stone image. Then Mitrānanda said to the merchant: 'My lord, who had this temple made? Who was the workman employed on it? Who had so much artistic skill? Did he make this statue by his own artistic invention only, or did he carve it to represent some person?' The merchant said: 'I had this temple made. It was made by an architect residing in the city of Sopāra, named Sūradeva.' Mitrānanda said: 'I will go to that city.' Then Amaradatta said: 'Without you I cannot support my life.' Then Mitrānanda crossed the sea, and went to the city of Sopāra. *There he put on a splendid garment, and, taking a present in his hand*, went to the architect's house. The architect showed him great regard, and asked him the cause of his coming. Mitrānanda said: 'I wish to have a temple built in honour of a god, therefore I have come to you. So show me a model of a temple.' The architect said: 'I made the temple in the garden outside Pātaliputra; this is the model of it.' Mitrānanda said: 'Was the marble statue in that temple devised out of your own head, or is it the likeness of any lady?' The architect said: 'The statue is copied from

Ratnamarijarī, the daughter of King Matrāsena in Ujjayinī, and is not the product of my own artistic invention.' When Mitrānanda heard this, he said: 'I will come to you again in an auspicious moment'; and thereupon he journeyed to Ujjayinī."*

The rest of the story, relating the manner in which Mitrānanda won the fair lady for his friend, does not concern us here; suffice it to say, that in the end "Amaradatta made Mitrānanda head of his cabinet, Ratnamanjarī was the jewel of his harem, and the merchant Ratnasāgara was appointed royal merchant."

As regards the organisation of craftsmen in villages, conditions were not, of course, identical in mediæval Ceylon, but they were, and to a large extent still are, similar in many ways. In 1872, out of 117 villages in the district of Nuvara Kalāviya, four were smiths' villages, and five potters' villages, occupied by persons of those castes exclusively; the extent of these amounted to 80½ acres in a total of 790 acres.†

In the Kandyan provinces, there existed a larger number of such villages, and also villages wholly or partly occupied by goldsmiths and other superior

---

* *Katha-kosa, translated by C. H. Tawney, p.* 150.

† *Service Tenures Commission Report, Colombo,* 1872, *p.* 487.

craftsmen. There were also whole villages granted to craftsmen and their descendants for ever, as *bada-vedilla*, or means of subsistence. The word *galladda*, a designation of craftsmen of the superior division, actually means "one who possesses a village"—a point of much significance in a study of the economic status of the Indian craftsman.

In Southern India the skilled craftsmen, exclusive, that is, of potters and weavers, are known as the *kammalar*. The following account of these craftsmen is partly based on a paper by Dr. Pulney Andy in No. 50, "Journal of Indian Art and Industry."

The *kammalar* are descendants of Aryans who entered India across the Panjab in early times, when they were known as Visva or Deva Brāhmans or Deva Kammālar. They spread gradually towards the south, and thence reached Ceylon, Burma, Siam and Java. The *kammalar* claim to have been at one time spiritual guides and priests to the whole people, of which position a trace survives in the saying, "The kammālan is guru to the world." They still have their own priests, and do not rely on Brāhmans; they also perform priestly rites in connection with the consecration of images. They both claim and possess various special privileges, which they have always upheld with much vigour; in some cases they claim a rank equal to that of Brāhmans. They are, or were, learned in the *silpa* *sastra*, or technical works on art in Sanskrit; the priests especially studied these books. But most they were only, in later times at least, known in word for word glosses in the vernacular. The *kammalar* trace their ancestry to the five sons of Visvakarma, of whom the first-born, Manu, worked in iron; the second, Maya, in wood; the third, Tvastram, in brass, copper, and alloys; the fourth, Silpi, in stone; and the fifth, Visvajna, was a gold and silver smith and jeweller. In former times the *kammalar* had their own guilds which protected their interests; but as these institutions gradually declined, they have been driven to seek the aid of capitalists of other castes, and now they are in a majority of instances reduced to mere paid workmen, earning daily wages. The five occupational sects form one compact community, and are not mutually exclusive; the son of any one may follow any of the five crafts at will. Probably many individuals practised more than one craft, as is still the case in Ceylon,* amongst the *navandanno*, who correspond in position to the *kammalar*, and in many instances are the descendants of *kammalar* immigrants. The group of castes corresponding to the *kammalar* in Mysore is called *Panchvala*.

* *So also in North Jaipur, carpenters worked not only in wood, but in stone, or metal, including gold, as might be required of them.—Col. Hendley, Indian Jewellery, p.* 153.

## CHAPTER IV.

### STANDARD AND REGULATION.

ROBERT KNOX, whose book, published in 1682, is still the best written and most interesting account of Ceylon, gives an amusing account of the craftsmen, incidentally mentioning an interesting form of *regulation* whereby to each smith a monopoly of the work in a special district was reserved.

"These Smiths," he says, "take much upon them, especially those who are the King's Smiths; that is, such who live in the King's Towns, and do his work. They have this Privilege, that each has a parcel of Towns belonging to them, whom none but they are to work for. The ordinary work they do for them is mending their Tools, for which every man pays to his Smith a certain Rate of Corn in Harvest time according to ancient Custom. But if any has work extraordinary, as making new tools or the like, beside the aforesaid Rate of Corn, he must pay him for it. In order to this, they come in an humble manner to the Smith with a Present, being Rice, Hens, and other sorts of provision, or a bottle of Rack, desiring him to appoint his time when they shall come to have their work done. Which when he hath appointed them, they come at the set time and bring both Coals and Irons with them. The Smith sits very gravely upon his stool, his Anvil before him, with his left hand towards the forge, and a little Hammer in his Right. They themselves who come with their work must blow the Bellows, and when the Iron is to be beaten with the great Maul, he holds it, still sitting upon his Stool, and they must hammer it themselves, he only with his little Hammer knocking it sometimes into fashion. And if it be anything to be filed, he makes them go themselves and grind it upon a Stone, that his labour of filing may be the less; and when they have done it as well as they can, he goes over it again with his file and finisheth it. That which makes these Smiths thus stately is because the Towns People are compelled to go to their own Smith, and none else. And if they should, that Smith is liable to pay Damages that should work for any in another Smith's jurisdiction."*

Of the King's Towns, or Royal Manors in Ceylon, Knox says also: "In each of these Towns there is a *Smith* to make and mend the Tools of them to whom the King hath granted them, and a *Potter* to fit them with earthenware, and a *Washer* to wash their Cloaths, and other men to supply what they

* *Cf. Appendix VII.*

have need of. And each one of these hath a piece of land for this their service, whether it be to the King or the lord; but what they do for the other People they are paid for. Thus all that have any Place or Employment under the King, are paid without any charge to the King."

A special feature of the guild activity has been alluded to already, in the statement that no unqualified person could remain in or enter it. It was, indeed, one of the most important functions of the guild in India, as in Europe, to maintain the *Standard* of quality, both of material and design. A forlorn trace of this survives in Europe in the hall-marking of gold and silver; and even that is not concerned with quality of design. In other cases the king or the State became responsible for the regulation of the craft sometimes in connection with the necessity for effective means of collecting the tolls and dues. The principle of *Regulation* is recognized in that fascinating and, for the study of Indian society, all-important law-book, the "Ordinances of Manu":

"He who avoids a custom-house, he who buys or sells at an improper time, or he who makes a false statement in enumerating his goods, shall be fined eight times the amount of duty which he tried to evade. Let the king fix the rates for the purchase and sale of all marketable goods, having duly considered whence they come, whither they go, how long they have been kept, the probable profit and the probable outlay. Once in five nights, or at the close of each fortnight, let the king publicly settle the prices of the merchants."

Here we see recognized the important doctrine of the "fair price," so striking a feature of the commercial ideas of Mediæval Europe. The commercial morality of the individual is also safeguarded:

"A weaver who has received ten *palas* of thread, shall return cloth weighing one *pala* more; he who acts differently shall be compelled to pay a fine of twelve *panas*. . . . All weights and measures must be duly marked, and once in six months let the king re-examine them."

Closely bound up with these arrangements is the system of taxation, which amounts to what we should now call an income tax, or more exactly, a royalty, the due contribution from the trader to the State which protects him and the king his patron, and here also we see provision for the estimation of the fair price:

"Let the king take one-twentieth of that amount which men well acquainted with the settlement of tolls and duties, and skilful in estimating the value of all kinds of merchandise, may fix as the value for each saleable commodity."

So also Yājnavalkya, 1360:

"A king, having duly corrected the castes, families, guilds of artisans (*sreni*), schools and communities of people that have swerved from the duty of their caste (*sva-dharmat*), should place them in the right path."

Let us examine a few instances of these commercial principles at work in India.

In the time of Chandragupta (3rd cent. B.C.) there were six Municipal Boards in Pātaliputra, of which the first was entrusted with the superintendence of everything relating to the industrial arts: fixing the rate of wages, and enforcing the use of pure and sound materials, as well as the performance of a fair day's work for fair wages. These boards consisted of five members each, and may be regarded as a development on official lines, of the ordinary *pancayat* or committee of five members by which every caste and trade in India has been accustomed to regulate its internal affairs from time immemorial.* The State regulation of craft appears to have been connected with the collection of tolls and revenues, and the two things hung together.

A reference to guilds and regulations is found in the *Ain-i-Akbari*, or Institutes of Akbar (sixteenth century), in the chapter dealing with the duties of the *Kotwal*, or City Officer.

* *Vincent Smith, "Early History of India," Ed. II., p.* 125.

"Out of each class of artificers he shall select one to be at their head, and appoint another their broker for buying and selling, and regulate the business of the class by their reports; and they shall regularly furnish him with journals attested by their respective seals. . . . He shall see that the market prices are moderate, and not suffer anyone to go out of the city to purchase grain; neither shall he allow the rich to buy more than is necessary for their own consumption."*

To this day the citizens of Srinagar lament the prosperous days of old, when the trade was not free, as it is now is.

"They have a common saying to the effect that when the taxation went the prosperity of the city went also, and they explain this by the fact that the removal of taxation led to the breaking up of what were practically guilds sanctioned and protected by the State. When the taxation was removed outsiders rushed in, and competition at once reduced prices of art wares. Copper-work, which sold at seven rupees per seer in the days of taxation, now sells at three rupees, and this is the case with many other art wares."

In the days of taxation also:

"The State exercised a vigorous supervision over the quality of the raw material and the manufac-

---

* *Ayeen Akbery, F. Gladwin*, 1800.

tured article. In the good days of the shawl-trade no spurious wool was brought in from Amritsar to be mixed with the real shawl-wool of Central Asia, and *woe betide the weaver who did bad work or the silversmith who was too liberal with his alloy. There is no such supervision nowadays.* Competition has lowered prices, and the real masters of weaving, silver, papier-maché and copper-work have to bend to the times and supply their customers with cheap, inferior work. Ask an old artist in papier-maché to show the work which formerly went to Kabul, and he will show something very different from the miserable trash which is now sold. But the Pathans of Kabul paid the price of good work ; the visitors to the valley want cheap work, and they get it."*

And so the story goes on. Let us take another case. Says Sir George Birdwood :

"Formerly, . . . a great industry in gold embroidered shoes flourished at Lucknow. They were in demand all over India, for the native kings of Oudh would not allow the shoemakers to use any but pure gold wire on them. But when we annexed the kingdom, all such restrictions were removed, and the bazaars of Oudh were at once flooded with the pinchbeck embroidered shoes of Delhi, and the

---

* *Sir W. Lawrence, "The Valley of Kashmir," p.* 373. *The italics are not in the original.*

Lucknow shoemakers were swept away for ever by the besom of free trade."†

And thus we see at work the degradation of standard, which is undermining alike the crafts of the East and of the West. "Under British rule," says Sir George Birdwood, "the authority of the trade guilds in India has necessarily been relaxed, to the marked detriment of those handicrafts the perfection of which depends on hereditary processes and skill." Modern individualism, in fact, whether we call it "Laissez Faire" in Manchester, or the introduction of "Free Western Institutions" into India, hesitates to interfere with a man's sacred individual liberty to make things as badly as he likes, and to undermine the trade of his fellows on that basis—a basis of competition in cheapness, not in excellence; and the result we know. Surely a strange product of civilization this!

Perhaps it is necessary to explain that in thus contrasting "Free Trade" with the status of "protected" industries, I do not intend at all to advocate "Protection" as commonly understood. The "Protection" which is here advocated is the *protection of standard*; this must be carried out in most cases *not by the taxation of imports*, but by the *absolute prohibition of the importation of any goods whose quality falls below the standard established*. The

† "*Industrial Arts of India*," *II.*, *p.* 64.

hall-marking of gold and silver is almost the only survival of this power formerly exercised by the trade guilds in England, and here it is only quality of material that is considered, not of design. In recent times, the principle has been put in practice in the prohibition of aniline dyes by Kashmir. The principle, however, requires great extension, if standard is to be maintained; and it is best done by restoring to the guilds that power of control which they formerly possessed. For the State to merely tax, and profit by, the importation of the inferior goods—"Protection" as ordinarily understood—would be quite futile from the present point of view. Equally foolish would be the taxation of goods which for one reason or another can better be made in another country than one's own. Each country should excel in its own special productions, and protect their standard ruthlessly.

## CHAPTER V.

### RELIGIOUS IDEAS IN CRAFTSMANSHIP.

THERE is another kind of provisi craftsman as society tending to secure the m a baron, or standard in the crafts. I allude to the c called dark some aspects of which we must consi patronage of here speaking of the origin and general course, and of caste, it will suffice to say from our po craftsmen. that it represents a legal recognition of who knew division of society into functional gro Even Alfred tically, there are four castes only, protecting his or learned caste; the *Kshattriya*, o craftsmanship statesmen; the *Vaisya*, or traders, c and we are craftsmen; and the *Sudra*, craftsmen a bears the Much subdivision and multiplication interest in has taken place, so that there are large num that widely distributed, but self-contained com should in India, whose members do not inter-ma evidence together. Caste is hereditary, that is to the West man is, and must remain, of the caste i" Mabin- he is born, and this is true even if he sl hall and the special occupation which is the tradit said the of his caste. There is a certain connection the caste and the guild, that is to say, the trade guild consists usually of persons of the same ethnic and sectarian caste; but when the same trade is pursued by men of different castes, as sometimes, but not often, happens, the guild may include all without reference to caste. The craftsman has always his caste, but is not always associated with others into a guild; the guilds are mainly confined to the great polytechnic cities, while the village craftsman stands alone. Yet even he is not alone, for he is a member of a great fraternity, the caste; and how much this means to him, it would be difficult to exaggerate. It means at once his pride and his duty (*dharma*). Caste is a system of *noblesse oblige*; each man is born to his ordained work, through which alone he can spiritually progress. This religious conception of a man's trade or profession as the heaven-ordained work of his caste, may best, perhaps, be likened to the honour of mediæval knighthood. For the priest, learning; for the king, excellence in kingcraft; for the craftsman, skill and faithfulness; for the servant, service. The way and the life are various, but progress is possible alone each in his own way: "Better is one's own duty even without distinction, than the duty of another, even with excellence; in another's duty danger lies." And so it is that for each, culture comes in life itself, not as a thing separate from life.

Take the *Vaisya* for example ; he is to be a grazier or a trader : he must, says Manu :

"Know the respective value of gems, of pearls, of coral, of metals, of woven stuffs, of perfume, and of condiments. He must be acquainted with the manner of sowing seeds, and of the good and bad qualities of fields, and he must perfectly know all measures and weights. Moreover, the excellence and defects of commodities, the advantages and disadvantages of different countries, the probable profit and loss on merchandise, and the means of properly rearing cattle. He must be acquainted with the proper wages of servants, with the various languages of men, with the manner of keeping goods, and the rules of purchase and sale. Let him exert himself to the utmost in order to increase his property in a righteous manner*, and let him zealously give food to all created beings."

Thus each man had not only an economic, but a spiritual status in society ; national righteousness is often described by saying that "each man lived according to the *dharma* of his caste, down even to the dancing girl who excelled in the duties of her calling also."

The doctrine of *Karma*, the strongest, perhaps, of all sanctions for morality, has something to do also

* *Cf., the saying of the Tamil poetess Auvvai, "What is acquired without wrong-doing is wealth."*

with craftsmanship. A man's deeds follow him as a cart follows the ox; whatsoever a man does will react upon himself, sooner or later, in this life or another; as a man sows, so also shall he reap. These ideas are rather quaintly expressed in some of the technical books of the craftsmen. Here, for instance, are some verses from the *Mayamataya*, speaking of good and evil craftsmen, and their fate in this life and in lives to come:

"Builders that build houses thus, after their death, will be re-born in a royal family; painters, if they make images accordingly, in noble families; cunning and skilful builders, though they should die, are friends of mine, for as they do, they become rulers and nobles, such is the old saying of the sages. One who knows amiss his craft, taking hire wrongfully, the which wife and children eat and enjoy, bringing misfortune on the owner of the house, that builder will fall into hell and suffer—these sayings are in *Mayamataya*, what remedy can there be then, O builders? There are men who make images of Buddha, though knowing naught of their craft; put no faith in what they say. Builders and painters both, who know naught of their craft, when hire is given according to the work accomplished, take that money and (leaving their work) rush home therewith; though they get thousands, there is nothing even for a meal, they have not so much as a piece of cloth to wear, that is the reward of past births, as you know; dying, they fall into hell and suffer pain a hundred lacs of years; if they escape they will possess a deformed body, and live in great distress; when born as a man, it will be as a needy builder; the painter's eyes will squint—look ye, what livelihood can there be for him? Builders who know their business well will become *rajas* lacking nought, so also cunning painters are meet to become nobles. Builders and painters taking money falsely from other men, thereby grow poor, so ancient sages have declared and shewn; doubt not this saying was in the *Mayamataya* book of sages lore; therefore, let builders and painters study *Mayamataya*: misfortunes ensuing in this world and the next are told of in its stanzas, behold how excellently."

A few more words may be said as to the craftsman's religious conception of his craft.* I do not refer to the application of the craft to religious ends, but to the conception of its intrinsic religiousness. In "pagan" lands, there is no hard line drawn between the secular and the religious things in life; religion is not so much a formula, as a way of looking at things, and so all the work of life may be a sacrament, may be done as it were unto the Lord.†

* *Appendix VI.*

† *In this connection, it is interesting to quote from so modern a work as Baha u'llah's 'Words of Paradise'*

Hindu craftsmen in certain parts of India "worship" the implements of their labour at the Dasahrā festival. This Hindu custom has survived amongst some Muhammadan converts, *e.g.*, the *thavais* of Northern India, who worship their tools at the *Id al-gitr*, making offerings of sweetmeats to them.† In Gwalior, in the modern State workshops, the workmen prepare models of trains, machinery, etc., on which they have been engaged and pay honour to these at the Dasahrā festival.

There is a God of the arts and crafts, whose name is Visvakarma, who is described as the 'lord of the arts, the carpenter of the gods, the fashioner of all ornaments, who formed the celestial chariots of the deities, on whose craft men subsist, and whom, a a great and immortal god, they continually worship.' The Indian craftsmen, or, at least, the most

---

*the following pronouncement: "It is incumbent on every one of you to engage in some employment such as arts, trades, and the like. We have made this, your occupation, identical with the worship of God, the True God." Compare with this conception of a man's life-work the following modern teaching of the Soto School of Buddhists in Japan: "Not only the building of a bridge or the provision of a ferry-boat is a work of charity, but so are all forms of benefiting life, commercial and industrial."—Rep. Third Int. Con. Religions, Oxford,* 1908, *I., pp.* 324, 153.

† *Arnold, Hindu Survivals among Indian Muslims, Rep. III. Int. Con. Relig.*, 1908, *I.*, 319.

important guild or caste of craftsmen, claim to be descended from the five sons of this deity, of whom one was a blacksmith, the second a carpenter, the third a founder, the fourth a mason, and the fifth a goldsmith; and the followers of these crafts in Southern India form still one compact community.

We find some curious and suggestive mystical ideas, not without practical applications, associated with the personality of the craftsman. His work is regarded rather as a sacred mystery, as a sacrament, than as a secular "trade." In illustration of this I quote an extract from the *Srimahavajrabhairava-tantra*, translated from the German version of Grünwedel*:

"The painter must be a good man, no sluggard, not given to anger, holy, learned, self-controlled, devout and charitable, free from avarice—such should be his character. The hand of such a painter may paint on Sura-cloth. Would he attain to success, then enters the gift of the Sura into him. He should draw his design in secrecy, after having laid the cloth quite flat. He may paint if besides the painter only a *sadhaka* be present, but not if a man of the world be looking on."†

* "*Mythologie des Buddhismus*," *p.* 102.

† *Interesting, though unfortunately abbreviated, details of the ritual preparation of the painter or imager for his work are given by Foucher, 'L'Iconographie Bouddhique de l' Inde,' II., pp.* 7–14.

# VISVAKARMA.

The Indian craftsman conceives of his art, not as the accumulated skill of ages, but as originating in the divine skill of *Visvakarma*, and revealed by him. Beauty, rhythm, proportion, idea have an absolute existence on an ideal plane, where all who seek may find. The reality of things exists in the mind, not in the detail of their appearance to the eye. Their inward inspiration upon which the Indian artist is taught to rely, appearing like the still small voice of a god, that god was conceived of as Visvakarma.† He may be thought of as that part of divinity which is conditioned by a special relation to artistic expression ; or in another way, as the sum total of consciousness, the group soul of the individual craftsmen of all times and places. Thus, king Duttha Gāmanī having enquired of a master bricklayer in what form he proposed to build the monument required, it is stated that "at that instant Visvakarma inspired him. The bricklayer, filling a golden dish with water, and taking some water in the palm of his hand, dashed it against the water in the dish ; a great globule, like a ball of crystal, rose to the surface ; and he said, 'I will construct it in this form.'" It is added that the delighted rāja bestowed upon him a suit of clothes

---

*The subject, however, belongs rather to the domains of art-philosophy and mysticism than to that of the craftsman, socially considered.* † *Cf., Appendix VI.*

worth a thousand pieces, a splendid pair of slippers, and twelve thousand pieces of money.*

All this is an expression of a religious conception of life, and we see the working of such ideas in actual practice. A few years ago a reproduction was made of a room in a palace belonging to the Mahārāja of Bhavnagar. The head carpenter was ordered to follow the ancient rules of his craft. As the work progressed, he observed that the finger of God was pointing the way, and that accordingly mistakes were impossible. In support of this, he quoted the ancient rules of his craft.

" The breadth of the room should be divided into twenty-four parts, of which fourteen in the middle and two at each end should be left blank, while the remaining two portions should each form windows or *jalis*. The space between the plinth and upper floor should be divided into nine parts, of which one should be taken up by the base of the pillar, six parts by the column, one by the capital, and one by the beam over it. He then added that should any departure be made from these rules, the ruin of the architect and death of the owner were sure to follow."†

The science of house building, says the *Brihat Samhita*, " has come down to us from the *Rishis* (sages), who obtained it from *Brahma*."

* *Mahavamsa, Ch. XXX.*

† *Sir George Watt, " Indian Art at Delhi."*

Can we wonder that a beautiful and dignified architecture is wrought in such a wise, and can such conceptions fail to produce serenity and dignity in life itself? Under such conditions, the craftsman is not an individual expressing individual whims, but a part of the universe, giving expression to ideals of eternal beauty and unchanging laws, even as do the trees and flowers whose natural and less ordered beauty is no less God-given. The old-fashioned Eastern craftsman speaks with more than a touch of scorn of those who "draw after their own vain imagining," and there is much to justify his view.

Finally, I give an account of the ceremony of painting the eyes of an image, as performed in Ceylon as illustrating a gorgeous and beautiful episode in the craftsman's life, and showing him in the performance of priestly functions. I omit many details, more fully related in my "Mediæval Sinhalese Art." The ceremony, being the concluding episode in the construction or redecoration of a temple, often occupying several years, and an occasion graced by the presence of the patron of the work, in many cases the king himself, was an occasion of general rejoicing and festivity. Crowds of men and women from neighbouring villages, dressed in white cloths, and bringing offerings of arecanut flowers, money, or other gifts to offer to the new image, or to the artists, found accommodation in temporary booths. In other booths were those who sold provisions. A *bana maduva*, or preaching hall, would be erected, and there would be much reading of *sutras* or Buddhist sermons. There would be abundance of white flags, music and dancing, gossip and edification.

Sometimes there was no royal patron, but the vihāra was erected by the subscriptions and assistance of the villagers themselves, who dedicated, with royal permission, small parcels of land for its maintenance. In one such case we read that the eager villagers were in such a hurry for their consecration festival, that they borrowed images from another temple for the occasion, before their own were ready. But let us suppose the king had ordered the temple to be erected by the state craftsmen of the court and district. The night before the ceremony the king and officers of the court, and often the ladies of the royal household, arrived, and found accommodation in special pavilions.

Ceremonies began with the recitation of the *Kosala Bimba Varnanava*, a legend of the making of a sandal-wood image of Buddha in his own time. Upon this followed the elaborate placing of eighty earthen pots, with offerings to Brahma and Vishnu, and the erection of altars to the regents of the eight points of the compass, with suitable offerings. Altars were also erected for the guardians of the door, whose images in ivory or wood had already been set on the jambs of the door of the image house, and an altar to the guardian of the site, the *genius loci*. These guardians of the temple are conceived of as pure and sweet natural powers, protectors of the shrine and guardians of the spiritual atmosphere about it. Within the temple an altar was erected to Gana Deviyō, and a rag figure prepared, afterwards to serve as a scapegoat to receive the first "glance" of the newly-painted eyes. All these arrangements were made by youths of the craftsman's caste, dressed as Brahmans. Another man, wearing a red dress, made the offerings, recited mantrams, and circumambulated the temple sun-wise. Tom-tomming and other music was kept up continuously.

The final ceremony took place at five a.m., in memory of Buddha's attainment of enlightenment at that hour so long ago in Kosala. The eyes of the image were painted by the king himself, or, in his absence, by the foreman craftsman in royal costume. The painter, accompanied by a second man, also robed, but less elaborately, and both with veiled heads, entered the temple, all others standing aloof. The second man carried the brushes, black paint, and a mirror. The latter was held before the image to receive its "glance." A white cloth was spread by the village washerman for the painters to walk on as they passed from door to image. While the painter put in the eyes, or, in some cases, separate sclerotics of crystal or other material were affixed, the second man recited Sanskrit charms, and held up the mirror. The ceremony was repeated for each image of Buddha or of the gods. Immediately on its completion the painter veiled his eyes, and thus blindfolded was led out and away to a vessel of water already prepared. Here he purified himself by bathing his head, repeating the Indian formula of water-consecration, "Hail, O ye Ganges, Godāvarī, Sarasvatī, Narmadā, Indus, and Kāverī, come and hallow this water." Then the painter cut the water with his sword, and the vessel was shattered. The painting of the eyes was deemed to be so sacramental, so great a mystery, that such purifications were needed to ensure immunity from evil that might fall upon the presumptuous mortal thus establishing a link 'twixt heaven and earth. Returning to the vihāra, the doors were opened. By this time the grey dawn had passed into day, and the sun was up. The patron and the foreman stood together on the threshold facing the people. The craftsman, repeating Sanskrit charms, sprinkled the people with water. The patron and the people then made offerings to the temple and to the craftsmen. The offerings of money, cloths, etc., made during a certain number of days, were set apart as perquisites of the craftsmen, in addition to the special remunerations already agreed upon, for in the case of important work, such as temple building, making of images, etc., payments in goods or money were agreed upon, in addition to the mere provision of sustenance during the progress of the work.

After such offerings, the people entered the temple to lay flowers on the altar and admire the paintings, with cries of *Sadhu*. After the festival had lasted several days, the people and craftsmen dispersed to their homes, the latter completing their purification by a *pirit* service—the only direct part in the proceedings taken by Buddhist priests. Throughout the rest of the ceremony all priestly offices had been performed by the craftsmen themselves, acting as Brāhman priests. The whole ceremony, though, here described in Ceylon, is essentially Hindu in character, and is typical of the sacerdotal functions of the Kammālar craftsmen. It is of necessity, from the nature of their work in making or repairing images, moreover, that the right of entry, otherwise belonging only to Brahmans, should be given to the craftsmen also. In some parts of Southern India they claim, and occasionally possess, a social prestige equal to that of Brāhmans. Otherwise, they would be classed as "good Sūdras," whose touch does not defile. It is said in Manu: "The hand of a craftsman engaged in his art is always ceremonially pure."

It is recorded in a Sinhalese grant of the early twentieth century that after such a ceremony as that described, the king (the last Kandyan king) appointed ecclesiastes for the temple service, and granted lands for its support, offering a palm leaf charter to the temple by laying it upon the altar.

Of the two manors dedicated, the king said that one was his mother's, and she joined in the offering. Then the royal group walked round the temple, and the king, seeing a bare space of rock, ordered the charter to be cut on the stone, and this was done; and it is there still. About two months later the king and his mother and sister visited the vihāra again, and the vizier read aloud the stone inscription, which was compared by the king with the original charter, in the presence of the chief priests, and praising the stone-cutters, he ordered them to be paid from the treasury.

And so in the old days religious architecture was the stronghold and foundation of the arts and crafts, and both together were fostered by successive kings, of whom it is said in the chronicle that they "were one with the religion and the people"; but what was all that to the Georgian Christian

Governor? What did he care for the religion, the music, or the art of a people so utterly alien to himself in culture and traditions? The royal craftsman found himself unsupported and unappreciated; and now, like so many other descendants of the Indian craftsmen, he is merely an agriculturist, perhaps even works on a tea estate, or he lives only to make brass trays and other pretty toys for passing tourists whose lives and manners he does not understand, and for whom, as he well knows by experience, any bungling is good enough, since they know nought of good or bad craftsmanship even in their own land, and still less in his.

And now, instead of the king going in the grey dawn with his mother and sister to be present at the consecration of a temple built by his minister and vizier, we see—the Governor, a mere five years' visitor, ignorant even of the people's language, much more so of their traditions and their ideals, as he goes with his English wife and her fashionable lady friends to open a bazaar in aid of the local missionary school for the daughters of Kandyan chiefs. Instead of the self-contained and independent village community, with its cultivated and forest lands, and its communal cultivation, there are the tea and rubber estates, and planters clamouring for a hut tax to induce the villager to work for them at profitable rates,—rates profitable, that is, to the canny shareholder away in England and Scotland; instead of the king's palace, we see the usual type of Government building, even uglier than in England, and a good deal more out of place; instead of the king's craftsmen, we see the government clerks, slaving away for a ten cents bonus for every error detected in somebody's accounts. O Sacred Efficiency, what things are done in thy name!

## CHAPTER VI.

### EDUCATION.

I HAVE spoken more than once of the "hereditary craftsman," a phrase justified by the hereditary fixity of social function under the caste system. But it is worth while to consider the point in greater detail. It is often assumed that the skill of the "hereditary craftsman" depends upon the direct inheritance of his father's individual skill. But this skill is an acquired character, and it is almost universally agreed by scientists that there is no such thing as the inheritance of an acquired character; a man who loses one leg does not have one-legged children; a man who learns to play well on the piano does not transmit that skill; nor can the craftsman transmit his acquired capacity for carving wood or chasing metal. On the other hand, of course, if it be supposed that large groups of craftsmen are descended from a common ancestor who originally possessed innate artistic genius (a different thing from actual skill in handicraft), it may be argued that this capacity is inherited, and this would be the case. Personally, I should be inclined to attach little value to the likelihood of the actual existence of such an ethnically superior race of craftsmen; one would think, indeed, that the absence of selection and elimination in an hereditary caste might lead rather to degeneration than to a preservation of standard. As a matter of fact, all these considerations are of small weight beside the question of education and environment, conditions of supreme importance, and implicit in the expression "hereditary craftsman" as ordinarily used. The important facts are these: *the young craftsman is brought up and educated in the actual workshop, and is the disciple of his father.* No technical education in the world can ever hope to compensate the craftsman for the loss of these conditions. In the workshop, technique is learnt from the beginning, and in relation to real things and real problems, and primarily by service, personal attendance on the master. And it is not only technique that is learnt; in the workshop there is life itself, that gives to the pupil both culture and metaphysics, more essential to art than technique itself; for what use is it to speak well if you have nothing worth saying? I have been struck, in contrast, by the inefficiency of the great Technical Schools in London, the pride of the County Council. Their watchword, like that of the

British in the East, is indeed efficiency; but this means that the Professor is hauled up before a committee if he is late in attendance, not that his personality is a first consideration.* It means, too, that he is expected to be intensely practical, and to go through some curriculum leading to certificates and prizes; woe betide him if he should waste time in giving to his pupils a metaphysic or teaching them mediæval romance. Small wonder that the pupils of these schools have so little to say; they cannot, indeed, put more into their work than there is in themselves. But in speaking of the Eastern system of craft education, I used the term *disciple* advisedly; for in the East there is traditionally a

* *In this exaltation of administrative ability over creative gifts, which are much rarer and more precious, our institutions share the weakness which pervades our industrial establishments, where the manager or superintendent usually gets larger pay and is regarded as more important than the most expert craftsman. In both we see the same striving for a certain sort of efficiency and economy of operation, and for the attainment of a completely standarised product. This tends in both cases to the elimination of individuality and to sterility. . . . I would that there might be displayed in the administrative offices of every institution of higher education this testy remark, once made by an eminent scholar: "You cannot run a university as you would a saw-mill!"*

*Address by Prof. F. L. Nicholls to the American Association for the Advancement of Science,* 1908. *Nature, January* 14*th*, 1909.

peculiar relation of devotion between master and pupil, and it is thought that the master's secret, his real inward method, so to say, is best learnt by the pupil in devoted personal service; and so we get a beautiful and affectionate relation between the apprentice and the master, which is impossible in the case of the busy professor who attends a class at a Technical School for a few hours a week, and at other times, when engaged on real work, and dealing with real problems, has no connection with the pupils at all.

The master need not be the boy's father; he may be an elder brother, or even unrelated; but in any case, once chosen, he is the ideal of the pupil, from which he never wavers. There are often trade secrets, simple enough it may be, but valuable as much in the idea as in the fact; these the master reveals to the faithful pupil only after many days, and when he has proved himself worthy. Devotion and respect for the teacher remain throughout life; I have seen a man of thirty receive wages in the presence of an elder brother, his teacher, and hand them to him as the master with the gentlest possible respect and grace; and as gently and delicately they were received, and handed back, waiving the right to retain; and this same elder brother had an aged father, a great craftsman in his day, and he never returned home with wages without offering them to him in the same way. I have seen few things in East or West more suggestive of entire gentleness than these expressions of reverence for the teacher. I need not point out what a perfected instrument for the transmission of a living tradition such an education forms. And if, to return to the Technical School of to-day, one may make a suggestion, it would be this: that supposing the aim be to train up a generation of skilled and capable craftsmen, it were better to appoint living master craftsmen as the permanent servants of the community, endowed with an inalienable salary, or better, a house, and demand of them that they should carry out the public works undertaken by the community, and that they themselves should keep apprentices, choosing out of them one to be their successor in the position of Public Craftsman. Such a system would do more to produce skilled craftsmen, and to produce good work, than would twice the money spent on Technical Schools and on competitive design for great undertakings.*

There are few, if any, places in India where the traditional methods of instruction are maintained in every detail. But a brief account of the system as surviving in Ceylon, almost to the present

* *See A. J. Penty, "Restoration of the Guild System"; and C. R. Ashbee, "Craftsmanship in Competitive Industry," Campden,* 1908.

day, may be useful here. We may suppose that a young boy, son of a caste craftsman, has been apprenticed to, or is the son of a younger brother of the master and teacher. His attitude is one of discipleship and deep respect. If not a relation, he has been brought to the craftsman's home, with presents of betel leaves and perhaps an offering of money or cloth, and given into the master's charge. During his years of instruction he will live with and be fed and clothed by his master and teacher, and when at last his education is complete, be given the last secrets of the art and perhaps some heirloom or gift of a design drawn by a famous painter generations back.

The boy is given first a wooden panel, primed with a preparation of iron slag, quart sand, coconut-shell charcoal, tamarind seed, and the leaves of *Eclipta erecta*. Upon this panel he learns to draw, using as pencil a sea urchin spine or a piece of pointed wood.

It is of interest to note that this method of instruction is so far practically identical with the method of drawing on a primed panel, prescribed for beginners by Cennini.*

The forms drawn upon the panel are certain peculiar curves, gradually elaborated into very complex studies in applied ornament. Drawing

* *See translation by Mrs. Merrifield, London,* 1894.

from nature is never taught. After the hand and eye and memory have been trained in the use of the fundamental curves in this fashion, traditional ornament, repeating patterns, and the like are taught, then mythical animals and designs with men and beasts in them. The pupil is also taught to use the brush, and assists his master in practical work in temples, at first by grinding the colours and general personal service, then by priming the surfaces, applying a ground colour, and by preparing and taking care of brushes and pigments, and lastly, by filling in outlines sketched in by the master for completion by the pupil. Experience is thus gained in practical work. There is nothing *dilettante* about the young craftsman's education. It begins early and is exceedingly thorough.

While it is in progress he has, in addition to his ordinary education, to learn by heart various Sanskrit works on art, with their meaning. These technical works, composing what is called the *Silpa Sastra*, or "science of the arts," describe various kinds of images, the characters of mythical animals, the measurements of images and buildings, the kinds of jewellery proper for kings, the proportions of various tools and utensils.

A point of interest is the extreme simplicity of the craftsman's tools and methods. The painter's brushes, for example, are made of the awns of various grasses, of squirrels' hair, of roots, or fibre, and he is always able to replace them or modify them at need. The repousser's tools he makes himself to suit the work in hand, and he does not hesitate to make a new tool out of an old one for a special purpose. The value of this simplicity lies in the fact that the craftsman relies upon himself rather than upon his tools, and at the same time is completely master of them, adapting them exactly to the requirements of the moment. So with the pigments and mediums. There is no mystery, and success depends on thoroughness and patience rather than on any secrets of the trade.

It would be easy to give further details of technique and methods here, but the purpose of the present work being rather to portray the craftsman than to describe his work, the reader is referred for such details to such works as "Mediæval Sinhalese Art," by the present author, "Industrial Arts of India," by Sir George Birdwood, "Indian Art at Delhi," by Sir George Watt, and the pages of the "Journal of Indian Art and Industry." It may also be remarked that Mr. Percy Brown, Director of the School of Art in Lahore, has there collected a valuable series of exhibits illustrating the traditional methods of instruction in the various crafts still, or until recently, practised in the district. It is of the utmost importance that further work of this kind should be undertaken before it is too late. While anthropologists and sociologists are busy studying savage tribes, there is much of the organized life of the ancient civilizations slipping away for ever, which it is of far more importance to study and record.

To conclude with the craftsman himself: perhaps there is nothing more striking about his position in society, whether as a villager, a guildsman, or a feudal servant than this—the assurance of his position, and the assurance of his purpose and value. It is only in the absence of anxiety as to the immediate future, that that quality of leisure so characteristic of true works of art and craft can appear in them. The serenity and dignity of his life are things which we cannot overlook, as Sir George Birdwood says, if we are rightly to understand the Indian craftsman.

"He knows nothing of the desperate struggle for existence which oppresses the life and crushes the very soul out of the English working man. He has his assured place, inherited from father to son for a hundred generations, in the national church and state organization; while Nature provides him with everything to his hand, but the little food and less clothing he needs, and the simple tools of trade. . . . . This at once relieves him from an incalculable dead weight of cares, and enables him to give to his work, which is also a religious function, that contentment of mind, and leisure, and pride and pleasure in it for its own sake, which are essential to all artistic excellence."†

The craftsman had this leisure for thought, and even for dreaming, and his economic position made him secure against oppression or want. He had no need to accumulate wealth, and we do not find that the wage asked by the traditional craftsman in unspoilt districts to-day represents more than a bare living for self and family.

Too often we forget that industry, *per se*, is of little or no value to humanity, if the results are valueless. But the true craftsman will often work overtime if he is interested. I have had Sinhalese craftsmen who insisted on working by lamplight far into the night. But the same craftsmen demand the right on other occasions to come and go at their will, and it would be quite vain to expect any particular piece of work done within a fixed time. The artistic and the commercial methods are thus radically different; and the artistic result cannot be attained on commercial lines, nor *vice versa*.

The current rate of wages for all depended much more on the general cost of living than on the degree of skill required for this special craft or the other.

---

† *Sir George Birdwood, "Industrial Arts of India."*

The craft was much more a "calling" than a trade, and to this day Sinhalese craftsmen care more for congenial work, and personal appreciation, than for money payments. And as we have seen, in the most typical cases, the craftsman received no money wage at all, but was repaid in other ways. Many a British workman would be glad to exchange his money wage for such security and appreciation as belonged to the Sinhalese craftsman of a hundred years ago. Presents, indeed, were expected, even grants of land, but these were for faithfulness and excellence; not a payment at so much a yard or so much an hour for such and such kinds of work. For the work was art, not commerce, and it would have been as idle to demand that a carpet like the Ardebil carpet should be designed and made at so much per square foot, as to expect Academy pictures to be done in the same way; indeed, I think it would be more reasonable to sell these by the square yard, than to suppose that the works of the Mediæval Eastern craftsman could be valued in such a way.

If now, in conclusion, we endeavour to sum up the results to which we are led by this study of the Indian craftsman, and by a correlation of his position in society with that of the craftsman in periods of good production in the Western world, and in other parts of Asia, we find that no really great traditional art has ever been produced, except under the following conditions: Freedom of the craftsman from anxiety as to his daily bread; legal protection of the standard of work; his art not exploited for profit. These are the material conditions; even more important is that spiritual conception of the serious purpose of art, which we find expressed in the work of true craftsmen of whatever age or place, but perhaps more in India than anywhere else. In other words, it has only been when the craftsman has had the right to work, the right to work faithfully, a right to the due reward of his labour, and at the same time a conscious or subconscious faith in the social and spiritual significance of his work, that his art has possessed the elements of real greatness. And so we can hardly avoid the conclusion that these will always be conditions necessary for the production of fine art and craft.

# LIST OF APPENDICES.

## Appendix I.

### Sir George Birdwood on The Indian Village Potter.

"THE Indian potter's wheel is of the simplest and rudest kind. It is a horizontal fly-wheel, two or three feet in diameter, loaded heavily with clay round the rim, and put in motion by the hand; and once set spinning, it revolves for five or seven minutes with a perfectly true and steady motion. The clay to be moulded is heaped on the centre of the wheel, and the potter squats down on the ground before it. A few vigorous turns and away spins the wheel, round and round, and still and silent as a "sleeping" top, while at once the shapeless heap of clay begins to grow under the potter's hands into all sorts of faultless forms of archaic fictile art, which are carried off to be dried and baked as fast as they are thrown from the wheel. Any polishing is done by rubbing the baked jars and pots with a pebble. There is an immense demand for these water jars, cooking-pots, and earthen frying-pans and dishes. The Hindus have a religious prejudice against using an earthen vessel twice, and generally it is broken after the first pollution, and hence the demand for common earthenware in all Hindu families. There is an immense demand also for painted clay idols, which also are thrown away every day after being worshipped; and thus the potter, in virtue of his calling, is an hereditary officer in every Indian village. In the Dakhan the potter's field is just outside the village. Near the field is a heap of clay, and before it rise two or three stacks of pots and pans, while the verandah of his hut is filled with the smaller wares and painted images of the gods and epic heroes of the Ramayana and Mahabharata. He has to supply the entire village community with pitchers and cooking-pans and jars for storing grain and spices and salt, and to furnish travellers with any of these vessels they may require. Also, when the new corn begins to sprout, he has to take a water-jar to each field for the use of those engaged in watching the crop. But he is allowed to make bricks and tiles also, and for these he is paid, exclusively of his fees, which amount to between £4 and £5 a year. Altogether, he earns between £10 and £12 a year, and is passing rich with it. He enjoys, beside, the dignity of certain ceremonial and honorific offices. He bangs the big drum, and chants the hymns in honour of *Jami*, an incarnation of the great goddess *Bhavani*, at marriages; and at the *dowra*, or village harvest-home festivals, he prepares the *barbat*, or mutton stew. He is, in truth,.one of the most useful and respected members of the community, and in the happy religious organization village life there is no man happier than the hereditary potter, or *kumbar*.

"Are not these the conditions under which popular art and song have everywhere sprung, and which are everywhere found essential to the preservation of their pristine purity? To the Indian land and village system we owe altogether the hereditary cunning of the Hindu handicraftsman. It has created for him simple plenty, and a scheme of democratic life, in which all are co-ordinate parts of one undivided and indivisible whole, the provision and respect due to every man in it being enforced under the highest religious sanctions,- and every calling perpetuated from father to son by those cardinal obligations on which the whole hierarchy of Hinduism hinges. India has undergone more religious and political revolutions than any other country in the world; but the village communities remain in full municipal vigour all over the peninsula. Scythian, Greek, Saracen, Afghan, Mongol and Maratha have come down from the mountains, and Portugese, Dutch, English, French and Dane up out of its seas, and set up their successive dominations in the land; but the religious trade union villages have remained as little affected by their coming and going as a rock by the rising and falling of the tide; and there, at his daily work, has sat the hereditary village potter amid all these shocks and changes, steadfast and inchangeable for 3,000 years, Macedonian, Mongol, Maratha, Portugese, English, French and Dane of no more account to him than the broken potsherds lying round his wheel."

---

'*Industrial Arts of India*,' 1880.

## APPENDIX II.

### SIR GEORGE BIRDWOOD ON MACHINERY AND HANDICRAFT IN INDIA.

"WHAT is chiefly to be dreaded is the general introduction of machinery into India. We are just beginning in Europe to understand what things may be done by machinery, and what must be done by hand-work, if art is of the slightest consideration in the matter.

"But if, owing to the operation of certain economic causes, machinery were to be gradually introduced into India for the manufacture of its great traditional handicrafts, there would ensue an industrial revolution which, if not directed by an intelligent and instructed public opinion and the general prevalence of refined taste, would inevitably throw the traditional arts of the country into the same confusion of principles, and of their practical application to the objects of daily necessity, which has for three generations been the destruction of decorative art and of middle-class taste in England and North-Western Europe, and the United States of America.

"The social and moral evils of the introduction of machinery into India are likely to be still greater.

At present the industries of India are carried on all over the country, although hand-weaving is everywhere languishing in the unequal competition with Manchester and the Presidency Mills. But in every Indian village all the traditional handicrafts are still to be found at work.

"Outside the entrance of the single village street, on an exposed rise of ground, the hereditary potter sits by his wheel moulding the swift revolving clay by the natural curves of his hands. At the back of the houses, which form the low, irregular street, there are two or three looms at work in blue, and scarlet, and gold, the frames hanging between the accacia trees, the yellow flowers of which drop fast on the webs as they are being woven.

"In the street, the brass and coppersmiths are hammering away at their pots and pans, and further down, in the verandah of the rich man's house, is the jeweller working rupees and gold mohrs into fair jewellery, gold and silver ear-rings, and round tires like the moon, bracelets, and tablets, and nose-rings, and tinkling ornaments for the feet, taking his designs from the fruit and flowers around him, or from the traditional form represented in the paintings and carvings of the great temple, which rises over the grove of mangoes and palms at the end of the street above the lotus-covered village tank.

"At half-past three or four in the afternoon the whole street is lighted up by the moving robes of the women going down to draw water from the tank, each with two or three water-jars on her head; and so, while they are going and returning in single file, the scene glows like Titian's canvas, and moves like the stately procession of the Panathenaic frieze.

"Later, the men drive in the mild grey kine from the moaning plain, the looms are folded up, the coppersmiths are silent, the elders gather in the gate, the lights begin to glimmer in the fast-falling darkness, the feasting and the music are heard on every side, and late into the night the songs are sung from the Ramayana or Mahabharata.

"The next morning with sunrise, after the simple oblations and adorations performed in the open air before the houses, the same day begins again. This is the daily life going on all over Western India in the village communities of the Dekhan, among a people happy in their simple manners and frugal way of life, and in the culture derived from the grand epics of a religion in which they live and move, and have their daily being, and in which the highest expression of their literature, art, and civilization has been stereotyped for 3,000 years.

"But of late these handicraftsmen, for the sake of whose works the whole world has been ceaselessly pouring its bullion for 3,000 years into India, and who, for all the marvellous tissue and embroidery they have wrought, have polluted no rivers, deformed no pleasing prospects, nor poisoned any air ; whose skill and individuality the training of countless generations has developed to the highest perfection, these hereditary handicraftsmen are being everywhere gathered from their democratic village communities in hundreds and thousands into colossal mills of Bombay, to drudge in gangs for tempting wages, at manufacturing piece goods, in competition with Manchester, in the production of which they are no more intellectually and morally concerned than the grinder of a barrel organ in the tunes turned out from it.

"I do not mean to depreciate the proper functions of machines in modern civilization, but machinery should be the servant and never the master of men. It cannot minister to the beauty and pleasure of life, it can only be the slave of life's drudgery; and it should be kept rigorously in its place—in India as well as in England.

"When in England machinery is, by the force of cultivated taste and opinion, no longer allowed to intrude into the domain of art manufactures which belongs exclusively to the trained mind and hand of individual workmen, wealth will become more equally diffused throughout society, and the working classes, through the elevating influence of their daily work, and the growing respect for their talent, and skill, and culture will rise at once in social, civil and political position, raising the whole country to the highest classes with them; and Europe will learn to taste of some of that content and happiness in life which is to be still found in the Pagan East, as it was once found in Pagan Greece and Rome."*

* Sir George Birdwood ('*Industrial Arts of India,*' 1880.)

## Appendix III.

### William Morris on Commercial War.

"FOR so far reaching is this curse of commercial war that no country is safe from its ravages; the traditions of a thousand years fall before it in a month; it overruns a weak or semi-barbarous country, and whatsoever romance or pleasure or art existed there is trodden down in the mire of sordidness and ugliness; the Indian or Japanese craftsman may no longer ply his craft leisurely, working a few hours a day, in producing a maze of strange beauty on a piece of cloth; a steam-engine is set a-going at Manchester, and that victory over nature and a thousand stubborn difficulties is used for the base work of producing a sort of plaster of China clay and shoddy, and the Asiatic worker, if he is not starved to death outright, as plentifully happens, is driven himself into a factory to lower the wages of his Manchester brother worker, and nothing of character is left him except, most like, an accumulation of fear and hatred of that to him unaccountable evil, his English master. The South Sea Islander must leave his canoe-carving, his sweet rest, and his graceful dances, and become a slave of a slave: trousers, shoddy, rum, missionary and fatal disease—he must swallow all this civilisation in a lump, and neither himself nor we can help him now till social order displaces the hideous tyranny of gambling that has ruined him."*

---

* *William Morris, "Signs of Change," p.* 10.

## APPENDIX IV.

### E. B. HAVELL ON CRAFTSMANSHIP AND CULTURE.

"THE important part which craftsmen, more especially Oriental craftsmen, have always played in the world's history as missionaries of civilisation, culture, and religion, is not generally realised by bookmen. Even at the present day the Indian craftsman, deeply versed in his *Silpa Sastras*, learned in folk-lore and in national epic literature, is, though excluded from Indian universities—or, rather, on that account—far more highly cultured, intellectually and spiritually, than the average Indian graduate. In mediæval times the craftsman's intellectual influence, being creative and not merely assimilative, was at least as great as that of the priest and bookman."*

* *E. B. Havell*, "*Indian Sculpture and Painting*," *p*. 183.

## Appendix V.

### E. B. Havell on the Official Suppression of Indian Craftsmanship at the Present Day.

"INDIA still possesses a large body of trained craftsmen who practise the art of building on similar principles and produce similar results to those of the great mediæval builders of Europe. They enter no University, for Indian Universities were founded for supplying material for the official machinery, and make no provision for either art or religion. But their ancestors built the Taj, the shrines of Mount Abu, and countless other masterpieces; they constructed the Mogul palaces, public offices, irrigation works, and everything of practical utility that the art of building could provide.

"How does our departmentalism provide for these needs to-day? A certain number of young men with no training either in art or in craft, learn by heart certain formularies for calculating the maximum weight which an iron girder will bear, the smallest dimensions to which a wall can be reduced without collapsing, the cheapest rate at which a building can be constructed so as to bring it within the annual departmental budget. When a department has settled on paper the plan of the building it wants, one of these engineers with an archæological turn of mind puts on to it a "Gothic" or "Classic" front, according to departmental taste, and provides a certain scale of departmental decoration according to departmental rank and dignity. Then the hereditary Indian craftsman whose family has practised the art of building for untold centuries is brought in to learn the wisdom of the West by copying the departmental paper patterns. How bad the art becomes is, perhaps, difficult to be understood by those to whom an archæological solecism is more offensive than an artistic eyesore; but it is easy to explain how wasteful and extravagant the system really is. To build one of the latest and perhaps the best of these archæological structures in Calcutta, a large number of Indian caste-builders were employed. Many of them were both artists and craftsmen—they could design, build, and carve. The structural design had been settled for them departmentally, so they had no concern with that. There was also a considerable amount of ornament to be carved, but that also had been designed for them in proper departmental style, which happened to be Italian Renaissance, so they were not allowed to attempt that. Other men who had been trained in the European archæological style in Bombay were brought over to copy mechanically the paper patterns prepared for them. These men were paid two rupees a day each. Now there are at the present time in the Orissa district, not far from Calcutta, and famous for its splendid native architecture, a considerable number of masons and builders who, within the last twenty years, have designed and carried out architectural decoration comparable with that of our finest mediæval building in Europe, and infinitely more beautiful than the imitation Renaissance ornament of the building I have referred to. The average earning of these men is four annas a day, or one-eighth of the wages paid for executing the departmental decoration. They and their fellow-artists all over India are constantly in want of work, for departmentalism has no need of their services. Indian art cries out for bread ; we give it museums, exhibitions, and archæology."*

* *E. B. Havell, Nineteenth Century, June,* 1907.

## APPENDIX VI.

### LAFCADIO HEARN ON CRAFT GODS IN CEYLON.

"ANOTHER development of ancestor worship—the cult of gods presiding over crafts and callings—deserves special study. Unfortunately, we are as yet little informed upon the subject. Anciently this worship must have been more definitely ordered and maintained than it is now. Occupations were hereditary; artizans were grouped into guilds—perhaps one might even say castes—and each guild or caste then probably had its patron deity. In some cases the craft-gods may have been ancestors of Japanese craftsmen; in other cases they were perhaps of Korean or Chinese origin, ancestral gods of immigrant artizans, who brought their cults with them to Japan. Not much is known about them. But it is tolerably safe to assume that most, if not all of the guilds, were at one time religiously organised, and that apprentices were adopted not only in a craft, but into a cult. There were corporations of weavers, potters, carpenters, arrow-makers, bow-makers, smiths, boat-builders and other tradesmen; and the past religious organizations of these is suggested by the fact that certain occupations assume a religious character even to-day. For example, the carpenter still builds according to Shinto tradition: he dons a priestly costume at a certain stage of his work, performs rites, and chants invocations, and places the new house under the protection of the gods. But the occupation of the swordsmith was in old days the most sacred of the crafts: he worked in priestly garb, and practised Shinto rites of purification while engaged in the making of a good blade. Before his smithy was then suspended the rope of rice straw (*shime nawa*), which is the oldest symbol of Shinto; none even of his family might enter there, or speak to him; and he ate only of food cooked with holy fire."*

* Lafcadio Hearn, "*Japan*," 1905, *pp*. 138–139. *See also, for religious ceremonies performed by craftsmen*, "*Mediæval Sinhalese Art*."

## Appendix VII.

### Lafcadio Hearn on Craft Guilds in Japan.

"IN feudal times . . . all craftsmen and all labourers formed guilds and companies; and the discipline maintained by those guilds or companies prohibited competition as undertaken for purely personal advantage. Similar, or nearly similar forms of organization are maintained by artizans and labourers to-day; and the relation of any outside employer to skilled labour is regulated by the guild or company in the old communistic manner. Let us suppose, for instance, that you wish to have a good house built. For that undertaking, you will have to deal with a very intelligent class of skilled labour, for the Japanese house-carpenter may be ranked with the artist almost as much as with the artizan. You may apply to a building company, but, as a general rule, you will do better by applying to a master-carpenter, who combines in himself the functions of architect, contractor, and builder. In any event, you cannot select and hire workmen; guild regulations forbid.

You can only make your contract; and the master-carpenter, when his plans have been approved, will undertake all the rest—purchase and transport of material, hire of carpenters, plasterers, tilers, mat-makers, screen-fitters, brass-workers, stone-cutters, locksmiths and glaziers. For each master-carpenter represents much more than his own craft-guild: he has his clients in every trade related to house-building and house-furnishing, and you must not dream of trying to interfere with his claims and privileges. He builds your house according to contract; but that is only the beginning of the relation. You have really made with him an agreement which you must not break, without good and sufficient reason, for the rest of your life. Whatever afterwards may happen to any part of your house—walls, floor, ceiling, roof, foundation—you must arrange for repairs with him, never with anybody else. Should the roof leak, for instance, you must not send for the nearest tiler or tinsmith; if the plaster cracks, you must not send for a plasterer. The man who built your house holds himself responsible for its condition, and he is jealous of that responsibility: none but he has the right to send for the plasterer, the roofer, the tinsmith. If you interfere with that right, you may have some unpleasant surprises. If you make appeal to the law against that right, you will find that you can get no plasterer, carpenter, tiler or plasterer to work for you on any terms. Compromise is always possible, but the guilds will resent a needless appeal to the law. And after all, these craft-guilds are usually faithful performers, and well worth conciliating . . . Apprentices bound to a master-workman, were boarded, lodged, clothed, and even educated by their patron, with whom they might hope to pass the rest of their lives. But they were not paid wages until they had learnt the business or trade of their employer, and were fully capable of managing a business or workshop of their own. . . . These paternal and filial relations between employer and employed have helped to make life pleasant and labour cheerful; and the quality of all industrial production must suffer much when they disappear."*

---

* LAFCADIO HEARN, "*Japan, an Interpretation*," *pp.* 440–445.

*Note.—It is stated in the* "*Indian Trade Journal*" *for Feb.* 19, 1907, *that the Japanese, in preparing to compete with European nations for commercial prosperity, are showing a distinct reversion to former ways and methods. Amongst other things, steps were being taken to reorganise the old Trade Guilds. The* "*Trade Journal*" *comments:* "*As the various guilds grow in power and influence they will be able to dictate to European or American traders, unless the latter also enter into combination.*"

## APPENDIX VIII.

### SER MARCO POLO ON CRAFT GUILDS IN CHINA.

IT is stated in Yule's Marco Polo (1903, 3rd ed., II., 186), that in the great city of Kinsay there were twelve guilds of the different crafts. "The document aforesaid [description of the great city of Kinsay] also went on to state that there were in this city twelve guilds of the different crafts, and that each guild had 12,000 houses in the occupation of its workmen. Each of these houses contains at least twelve men, whilst some contain 20 and some 40—not that all these are masters, but inclusive of the journeymen who work under the masters. And yet all these craftsmen had full occupation, for many other cities of the kingdom are supplied from this city with what they require.

"The document aforesaid also stated that the number and wealth of the merchants, and the amount of goods that passed through their hands, was so enormous that no man could form a just estimate thereof. And I should have told you with regard to those masters of the different crafts who are at the head of such houses as I have mentioned, that neither they nor their wives ever touch a piece of work with their own hands, but live as nicely and delicately as if they were kings and queens. The wives, indeed, are most dainty and angelical creatures! Moreover, it was an ordinance laid down by the king that every man should follow his father's business, and no other, no matter if he possessed 100,000 beyants." It is also recorded that there were "officers appointed by the king to decide differences arising between merchants or other inhabitants of the quarter."

It is interesting to remark the following extract from Marco Polo's will: "I also bequeath . . . four *lire* to every guild or fraternity of which I am a member."

Yule's note on this is as follows:

"The word rendered *Guilds* is '*Scholarium.*' The crafts at Venice were united in corporations called *Fragliae*, or *Scholae*, each of which had its statutes, its head, called the *gastald*, and its place of meeting, under the patronage of some saint. These acted as societies of mutual aid, gave dowries to poor girls, caused masses to be celebrated for deceased members, joined in public religious processions, etc., nor could any craft be exercised except by members of such a guild." [*Roman*, I, 370.]

*Yule's Marco Polo, ed. 3, p. 72.*

## Appendix IX.

### Bhikku P. C. Jinavaravamsa on Craftsmen of Siam.

A FASCINATING account of Siamese craftsmen and their social organization is given by Bhikku P. C. Jinavaravamsa, in the *Ceylon National Review* for July, 1907. There were ten groups of artists and craftsmen organised under one State Department of Art and Craft. The ten groups consisted, briefly, of builders, wood-carvers (architectural), wood-carvers (small work), painters, imagers, gilders, stucco-workers, turners, repoussers, and goldsmiths. Twenty-eight other departments were separately constituted under chiefs or under one of the ten main departments according to the king's wishes. Amongst these were founders, puppet makers, tailors, goldsmiths, enamellers, tanners, inlayers with mother of pearl, makers of glazed pottery and tiles, stone-carvers, etc.

"Just as in mediæval Europe the art of decorative painting was taught in the ecclesiastical buildings; so here drawing and painting are taught in Buddhist temples; some branches are also taught in palaces.

"There is no such thing as a regular course of lessons or organized training among the different crafts. Examples are given by the master for the pupil to 'look at' and 'copy.' The master seems to criticise the pupil's work rather than direct him, and the pupil's endeavour is to imitate the master; this is the nature of the training. Apprentices are generally the master's own children or those of relatives or even neighbours; the pupils crowd round the work on which the master is engaged, and are told to 'watch' and to 'try to do the same,' and are employed in grinding and mixing colours and paints, and also help in handling the work and in any other labour connected with it. In this way I have learnt to do many things from my childhood.

"The only real *school* of arts and crafts is the residence of the head of the Department of Ten Crafts, where all kinds of work are almost always going on, and, in cases of working against time, by night as well as by day. Of course, only such kinds of work as are portable are done here, or work which can be done in sections and afterwards put together *in situ*, such as a bedstead.

"When any of the apprentices show aptitude for any particular craft, he is set to do the simplest work first, such as painting the ground, filling up spaces, washing in the sky and water, and finally tracing the outline of figures and other objects in the picture; illumination and shading are the last stage."

## CRAFTSMEN OF SIAM.

The following extracts are given to show the characteristic methods of the Oriental craftsman in Siam:

"In the case of water colour painting on a plaster surface, the surface is first sized with a decoction of tamarind seeds and leaves in two or three coats; the object of this is to neutralize the alkali and to make the surface firm and non-absorbent.

"The subject being decided upon (generally a jātaka, or the Rāmāyana, or some other popular legend), the master painter takes a selected piece of bamboo charcoal (or even a rough piece of charred wood), and proceeds to mark out by zigzag lines the divisions between successive scenes. Within the spaces thus marked out he next makes a rough sketch of the subject, and gradually develops it into a detailed drawing. Then he, or his best pupils, outline the figures or design in some dark colour, often the sediment of the water in which brushes are washed, with a lining-in brush, inserting all detail. The figures are then filled in with white paint, and the ground painted in with appropriate colours representing earth, sky or water. The figures are then finished in colour and detail added in red, or black, or gold. . . . The painter's tools consist merely of some half-a-dozen brushes made of the hair of cow's ears, bound in a crow or goose quill, two or three flat brushes made of bark, and a 'foot-rule' generally one cubit long, and sometimes divided into inches by mere saw-cuts.

"If the painting be of the nature of a regular pattern or consist of repeated figures, the artist resorts to perforated paper patterns. A thick native-made black paper is used, pieces being joined together if one is not large enough. The designer roughly sketches the pattern on it with a soft limestone pencil (greyish-white or light-yellow) cut to the required size and pointed at both ends. If it is necessary to rub out any lines, the artist uses his finger, moistened in the mouth, but if a large area is to be erased, a piece of the same paper, dipped in water, is used. When the design is thus completed, it is lined in in white with a fine brush; corrections can be made in black.

"The stencil thus made is placed on a cushion and closely pierced or pricked along the design with a needle. It is then ready for use. It is laid on the surface to be decorated, and which has been prepared, and powdered chalk (in a cloth bag of loose texture) is rubbed or dusted over it, so that the pattern appears on the prepared surface as a series of faint dotted lines.

"A special craft connected with painting is the art of making transparent pictures for what Europeans call, though incorrectly, 'shadow pantomime.' This is a show of moving transparent pictures over a screen illuminated by a strong bonfire behind. The scenes represent the favourite Indian drama of Rāmāyana, and are accompanied by music and intoned recitation, and sometimes singing. The method of preparation of these pictures is very interesting. A cowhide is scraped to the required thinness (generally about 1-16 inch), evenly stretched and allowed to dry hard. It is then roughly shaped—oval for a group and long rectangular for a standing figure—the pieces measuring generally from 2½ to 5 feet in height or diameter. A design is drawn on native-made black paper, perforated and transferred as already described, and then outlined in black upon the hide. Flame *kanaka* or other appropriate ornaments or flowers or trees are introduced to connect together the different pieces or projecting parts of a figure, so that when the ground is cut away the hide is held together by these connections and will also hang evenly without buckling. Sky or other open space is represented by small even patterns of a very open character with inconspicuous connections.

"The hide, after cutting in this way, is appropriately coloured with fast bright dyes which penetrate the leather, and are fixed by lime-juice or native vinegar, which help also to brighten the colour.

"The greatest difficulty is to estimate how much light will, as they say, 'eat up' the figure; for the appearance of the figure is altered by the light from behind, some colours being weakened and others intensified. If, for instance, a human figure is drawn (generally dark) in good proportion, with dress and ornament and the colour of hair and skin correctly represented, the picture will appear badly proportioned when lit up. The artist must be a man of great experience, and the worst of it is that he does not seem able to explain his art nor to set forth in black and white the proportion of this or that colour which will absorb or transmit the light most. It is amusing to see young artists' attempts at making these apparently simple transparent pictures, with thick white paper beautifully illuminated, but turning out a complete failure when exhibited. The pictures are held up before the screen by four pieces of split bamboo just strong enough for the purpose, and fastened to the picture, two in front and two behind, the lower ends serving as handles. The hide is flexible, so that it can be rolled up round the two sticks. The performer must be himself a trained dramatic artist and dancer to music. He acts the scene, as he would on the stage, with every part of his body except the two arms, engaged in holding up the picture. He seems to live in the picture, and is absorbed in the representation he is trying to produce. It is most amusing to see the artist's attitude and observe the very intense expression of his face as he performs and watches the motion of his picture. The same remarks apply to the puppet-show man described below.

"The puppet-shows also deserve some mention. The construction of moving figures and puppets is carried to a considerable degree of perfection. Beautiful little figures, 6 inches to 18 inches high, representing the characters of the Indian drama of Rāmāyana, are made for exhibition at royal entertainments. They are perfect pieces of mechanism; their very fingers can be moved and made to grasp an object, and they can be made to assume postures expressive of any action or emotion described in poetry. This is done by pulling strings which hang down within the clothing, or within a small tube attached to the lower part of the figure, with a ring or loop attached to the end of each, for inserting the fingers of the showman. The movements are perfectly timed to the music and recitation or singing.

"One cannot help being charmed by these lilliputs, whose dresses are so gorgeous and jewelled with the minutest detail. Little embroidered jackets and other pieces of dress, representing the magnificent robes of a Deva or Yakkha, are complete in the smallest particulars. The miniature jewels are sometimes made of real gold and gems.

"Such a thing as this I believe to be only possible when a man has almost unlimited means, both in time and money, to devote to his hobby for months (as was the case with the late and last so-called ‘second king,’ whose puppet-show was the most famous ever called into existence), to complete the work.

"In their artistic taste the Siamese seem to be guided by an instinctive appreciation of beauty, rather than a self-conscious striving after it. They understand form, and especially curves and their combinations, very well, and use them to advantage. They understand well the filling of space with appropriate ornament, so that odd or awkward spaces become restful and even, or form a contrast to the more ornamental part of the work, making it stand out clearly, fulfilling the function of light and shade in modern work. Composition, or the proper disposition of spaces is carefully studied—if the criticism one constantly hears passed upon this or the other work may be called study. The Siamese artists show accurate judgment of size and distance, light and level; men with such accurate judgment are called *ta jang*, *i.e.*, eye of an expert.

"An excellent artist is referred to as *nakleng* (hobbyist, connoisseur, 'well-trained'), and even when the term is applied in the case of bad habits, as to a connoisseur of good wines or to a gourmet, it is a complimentary term. It is also applied to collectors in general. It is, however, understood to imply a morally weak man, one who gives way to passion, but decidedly a jolly good fellow. A rowdy or immoral man, or one noted for quarrels, is also called *nakleng*, in a bad sense." *

---

* "*Ceylon National Review*," *No.* 4, 1907.

## APPENDIX X.

### MUNICIPAL INSTITUTIONS IN ANCIENT INDIA.

"According to Vrihaspati and Yājnavalkhya, villages, townships, guilds of merchants and mechanics, communities of Brāhmans, and heretics and other bodies should, when expecting common danger or when inspired by a desire to properly discharge their secular and religious duties, or those relating to their trade or profession, in the case of mercantile or other guilds, enter into an agreement among themselves for the protection of their common interest and the proper performance of their duties.

"The duties, specified under their agreements which these bodies were required to execute in writing, and which thereby acquired a moral and legal sanction, were the repair of public halls, *prapas* (places where drinking water is supplied to travellers, wells, cisterns, etc.), temples, tanks and gardens, the performance of the purificatory rites for the poor and the destitute, and arrangements for the cremations of dead paupers, distribution of gifts among the people desirous of performing religious acts, and supporting people in time of famine and distress.

"It is these duties which were known as *samuha-krita-sambit*, or the course of conduct or duty established by the public bodies.

"The *samuhas* were free to take up other duties also, provided that they were not inconsistent with, or antagonistic to, their main duties." *

"Headmen (commissioners) residing in towns and forts, and managing the affairs of *Pugas* (mercantile and other guilds), *Srenis* (bodies of men, following the same trade or profession), and *Ganas* (communities of Brāhmans or of other people distinct from the *Srenis*) should punish wrongdoers by administering rebuke or censure, as well as with social ostracism and banishment.

"And the favour or disfavour thus meted out by them (to the people), when in accordance with the precepts of religion and morality, should be accepted by the king; for general approval had already been accorded to whatever these might do (in the ordinary course of their duties)." †

---

* *Quoted by A. C. Das in "Modern Review," Vol. II.*, 1907, *p.* 182, *from a paper by Rai Bahadur Pandit R. C. Shashi, in the Buddhist Text Society's Journal.*

† *Translation of a text of Vrihaspati, quoted loc. cit.*

## Appendix XI.

### Books Recommended to the Reader.

The following books and articles are here mentioned, and specially recommended to the reader, as bearing, whether directly or indirectly, upon the subject of "The Indian Craftsman":

John Ruskin: "Unto This Last."
"The Nature of Gothic."
William Morris: "Architecture, Industry and Wealth."
A. J. Penty: "The Restoration of the Guild System."
C. R. Ashbee: "Craftsmanship in Competitive Industry," 1908.
A. K. Coomaraswamy: "Mediæval Sinhalese Art," 1908.
Sir George Birdwood: "Industrial Arts of India."
E. B. Havell:
"Indian Administration and 'Swadeshi,'" *Nineteenth Century*, July, 1907.
"Art, Ethics, and Economics in Hand-loom Weaving," *East and West*, August, 1907.
"Indian Sculpture and Painting," 1908.

THE END.

# Probsthain's Oriental Series.

**Buddhism as Religion: Its Historical Development and Present-Day Condition in all its Countries.**

By H. Hackmann, Lic. Theol. From the German, revised and enlarged by the Author. Translated by Miss Kemp. Crown 8vo, ca. 300 pages. Price, 5/- net. In press.

**The Masnavi, by Jalal al Din Rumi. Book the Second.**

Translated for the first time into English Prose, with a Commentary, by C. E. Wilson, B.A. (Lond.), Professor of Persian University College, London. 2 vols. Vol. I., Translation; Vol. II., Commentary. Price ca. 15/- net.

**Of the six books of the Masnavi,** only the first has hitherto been translated into English, by the late Sir James Redhouse, but it is not necessary to read the first book in order to understand the second and succeeding books, since the whole work is not a systematic and ordered treatise on Sufiism.

---

**ALWIS, JAS.—Descriptive Catalogue of Sanskrit, Pali and Singhalese Literary Works of Ceylon.** Vol. I. (all), 8vo, dp. xxx., 243. 1870. 9/-

**BAYNES, H.—The Idea of God and the Moral Sense in the Light of Language.** 8vo, pp. xiii., 239, 104. 1895. 10/6.

**BUDDHIST REVIEW, Organ of the Buddhist Society of Great Britain.** Vol. I. now in progress. 4/-

**DAWES, F.—Six Essays on the Ancients, their Music and Instruments.** I., Chinese, Japanese, Hindoos. 40, pp. 20. 1893. 2/6.

**EITEL, E. J.—Handbook of Chinese Buddhism,** being a Sanskrit-Chinese Dictionary, with Vocabularies of Buddhist Terms. 8vo, pp. 231. 1888. 18/-

**ERVAD, R. J. MEHERJIRANA.—Genealogy of the Naosari Parsi Priests.** 40 pp., xx., 194. 1907. 25/-

**GRIFFITHS, R. J., and Rogers, A.—In Persia's Golden Days** (Story of Kusru and Shirin). 8vo. 1889. 2/6.

**HAR BILAS SARDA.—Hindu Superiority. Attempt to determine the Position of the Hindu Race.** Royal 8vo, pp. xxxii., 454. Illus. 1907. **12/6.**

**KLIENE, CHAS.—Anglo-Chinese Calendar, A.D. 1751-2000.** 4vo, pp. vi., 500. Half-calf. 1906. **£2 2s.**

**LLOYD, A.—Admiral Togo: A Biography.** 8vo. Illus. 1905. **2/6. The Praises of Amida.** Buddhist Sermons translated from the Japanese. 8vo, 1907. **3/-**

**MASAYOSHI, COUNT.—Report on the Adoption of the Gold Standard in Japan.** Royal 8vo, pp. xv., 389. 1899. **14/-** **—Report on the Port Bellum Financial Administration in Japan, 1896-1900.** 8vo, pp. xviii., 256. 1901. **10/6.**

**MAYERS, Fr. W.—Treaties between the Empire of China and the Foreign Powers.** 8vo, pp. 354. 1906. **15/-**

**NIZAMI—Laili and Majnun.** Translated from the Persian by J. Atkinson and L. C. Byng. 8vo, pp. xxii., 162. 1905. **5/-**

**SPIEGEL, Fr. VON.—Iranian Art.** 8vo, pp. 59. 1886. **2/6.** **—and W. GEIGER—The Age of the Avesta and Zoroaster.** 8vo, pp. 149. 1886. **3/6.**

**STEVENS, H. J.—Cantonese Apothegms.** In Chinese with Translations and Commentary. 8vo, pp. iii, 155. 1902. **6/-**

**SUBHADRA BHIKSHU.—Buddhist Catechism.** 8vo, pp. iv., 75. 1908. **1/-**

**TEMPLE, R. C.—Dissertation on the Proper Names of the Panjabis.** 8vo, pp. viii., 228. 1883. **3/6.**

**WESTCOTT, G. H.—Kabir and the Kabir Panth.** 8vo, pp. vii., 185. Illus, 1907. **3/6.**

We have in the "Kabir Panth" an attempt to break down the barriers that separate Hindus from Mohammadans. "The Kabir Panth" is a religious system that owes something to Hindu, Mohammadan and Christian Influences.

---

*Published by*

**Facsimile Publisher**
Ashok Vihar, Delhi-110052 (India)
Website: www.facsimilepublisher.com

*Distributed by*

**Gyan Books Pvt. Ltd.**
5, Ansari Road, Daryaganj, New Delhi-110002 (India)
E-mail: books@gyanbooks.com, Website: www.gyanbooks.com

2 222000 008727